Women's Voice in Indian Fiction in English

Women's Voice in Indian Fiction in English

Edited by
Vijay Kumar Roy

ADHYAYAN

ADHYAYAN PUBLISHERS & DISTRIBUTORS
New Delhi-110002

Published by
ADHYAYAN PUBLISHERS & DISTRIBUTORS
4378/4B, 105, J.M.D. House, Murari Lal Street
Ansari Road Darya Ganj, New Delhi - 110002
Ph.: 011-23263018, 011-23277156, Fax: 23280028
Email: adhyayanpublishers@yahoo.com

Women's Voice in Indian Fiction in English

Edition 2011
ISBN 978-81-8435-275-7

Printed in India

Published by Harish Chandra Yadav for Adhyayan Publishers & Distributors, Delhi. Laser Typesetting at Jain Computers and Printed at Tarun Offset Printers. Delhi

Foreword

The present book entitled *Women's Voice in Indian Fiction in English* edited by Dr Vijay Kumar Roy is a welcome addition to the steadily growing critical interest in the field of Indian Writing in English in general and women's writing in the realm of fiction in particular.

The book contains fourteen well-argued critical papers dealing with some of the established and 'new' female novelists. As is well-known, some of the writers whose works have been discussed in detail and depth are celebrities such as Nayantara Sahgal and Anita Desai who surfaced in the late fifties or sixties, while some of them caught the attention of discerning readers with their appearance in the eighties or nineties. By now the novelists like Kamala Markandaya, Shashi Deshpande, Manju Kapur, Shobha De, Arundhati Roy, Kiran Desai and Anita Nair have carved out important places for them by virtue of their distinctive style and engagement with burning issues confronting the lives of women from various strata.

Obviously, the present book offers a mixed bag but what binds the book into a pattern is the basic theme that women writers have broken their long silence and defied the 'law of threshold'. They have demonstrated that women are no longer shy, diffident, vulnerable and a willing prey or victim of male prejudices or tyranny. They may lose the game or may sue for compromise but they are not going to surrender without a fight and at least in some cases, they are ready to survive on their own terms. Among the contributors, Anita Desai occupies the place of pride and justifiably so as she along with Nayantara Sahgal set the norm for Women's survival with dignity more often than not striking a balance between self and society.

As Nirmal Sharma has rightly argued, Anita Desai "depicts the Indian Woman as a fighter, a victim, a heroine and ultimately a winner because of her indomitable spirit and attitude of compromise."

Another contributor Kalpana Sharma in a joint paper with Sunidhi Bissa, has attempted a close textured analysis of Anita Desai's most well - known novel *Fire on the Mountain,* a Sahitya Akademi winner, and has demonstrated convincingly by studying the key images and symbols that alienation is an existential condition of sensitive and strong - willed women but withdrawal into silence does not offer an easy solution.

Narendra T. Mane's paper on Kamala Markandaya analyses the cultural clashes. It shows that the Indian culture and the alien culture are the two standpoints which will never meet together. What wide gap Markandaya experienced in England is the central theme of the paper.

As for the contributors dealing with the fiction of Shashi Deshpande, one of the finest successors of Ania Desai, the two articles provide a very intelligent analysis of the fiction of Shashi Deshpande.

To be specific, the article by Dalvir Singh Gahlawat is quite focused and incisive and it rightly highlights the "basic issues of power structure and role division in the patriarchal society of India". It is good to see that a male scholar has taken pains to realize that women's inferiority is not 'designed in heaven' but it is the creation of 'male dominated, gender biased society. He has made a chronological survey of the main novels of Shashi Deshpande and has shown the progress of women in their struggle for liberation through a dialectical process of revolt, defeat and survival. The contributor's concluding remark is quite convincing . "The new woman is inching towards freedom and she has been trying to learn bonding with one another."

Again in the two papers on Manju Kapur's novels viz. *Difficult Daughters* and *Home* the Contributors Indu Swami and Sudista Prasad Singh respectively have trodden familiar grounds and have come out with the conclusion that Manju Kapur's success as a novelist has to be viewed both from the points of view of partition and its damaging impact on women who are known to be makers of home and hearth.

In the first essay, the contributor has shown convincingly that partition has affected the psyche of women more than men. The first scholar portrays a woman's courage to stand on her feet and eke out her existence. The novel is both a path - breaking and myth breaking as it shows that the mother is not always a 'nurturing and fear dispelling presence' but as nagging restricting person. The contributor has rightly concentrated on three generations of women who inspite of their own suffering and agony, continue the myth of women's traditional role of motherhood and carrying out family obligations. The article by Sudista Prasad Singh, concentrates on Manju Kapur's next novel *Home.* The author rightly observes, "Manju Kapur has raised a very pertinent question of Women's identity especially after her marriage". There are a few interesting papers on Arundhati Roy, Kiran Desai and, of course, Anita Nair.

Arundhati Roy has been discussed too much and from several angles. In a joint paper, the contributors (Shakshi Tyagi and Sandeep Kumar) have raised the issue of treatment of Dalits (Paravans) in depth and detail. As for Kiran Desai's novel *The Inheritance of Loss,* the scholar (M. S. Wankhede) has shown convincingly that a number of allied themes bind the novel and issues like morality, justice, globalization, economic inequality, fundamentalism, and alienation are all mixed up. All characters in the novel suffer some kind of loss which is man's existential burden. The beauty of the novel lies in the novelist's suggestion that there are no easy solutions to the problems of pain and suffering.

Last but not the least, Shobha De's Feminism and Nayantara Sahgal's women oriented novels have been also taken up by two contributors. To the present reviewer both are good attempts at highlighting women's problems in a male dominated society.

On the whole the present offering of critical essays will spur other readers to come out with such serious and exclusive close reading of many other texts and female authors who have surfaced in recent years.

– Prof. P. S. Sanyal
University Professor of English (Retd.)
L. N. Mithila University, Darbhanga, Bihar.

List of Contributors

Vijay Kumar Roy, Assistant Professor of English, SRM University, NCR Campus, Modinagar, Ghaziabad, UP.

Ashok Kumar, Department of English Language, State Council of Educational Research and Training, Uttarakhand.

Narendra Tryambakrao Mane, Assistant Professor, Department of English, J. D. Patil Sangludkar Mahavidyalaya, Daryapur, Maharashtra.

Nirmal Sharma, Assistant Professor, Department of English, SRM University, NCR Campus, Modinagar, Ghaziabad, UP.

Kalpana Purohit, Associate Professor, Department of English, JNVU, Jodhpur, Rajasthan.

Sunidhi Bissa, Department of English, JNVU, Jodhpur, Rajasthan.

Dalvir Singh Gahlawat, Department of English, Singhania University, Rajasthan.

Arvind Kumar Sharma, Assistant Professor, Department of English, SRM University, NCR Campus, Modinagar, Ghaziabad, UP.

Suman Lata, Department of English, SRM University, NCR Campus, Modinagar, Ghaziabad, UP.

Laxman Yadav, Department of English, Patna University, Patna, Bihar.

Indu Swami, Department of English, Assam University, Diphu Campus, Diphu.

Sudista Prasad Singh, Head, Department of English, Samta College, Jandaha, Vaishali; B. R. A. Bihar University, Muzaffarpur, Bihar.

Sakshi Tyagi, Department of English, D. N. College, Meerut, Uttar Pradesh.

Sandeep Kumar, Department of English, Chaudhary Charan Singh University, Meerut, Uttar Pradesh.

Kumkum Bhardwaj, Professor and Head, Department of Humanities, Skyline Institute of Engineering and Technology, Greater Noida, UP.

Wankhede M. S., Associate Professor, Department of English, Dhanwate National College, Nagpur, Maharashtra.

Arun Kumar Mukhopadhyay, K.M.Institute, Bankura, West Bengal.

Pankaj Kumar 'Niraj', Lecturer, Department of English, Dr. J. M. College, Muzaffarpur, Bihar.

Contents

1

Introduction

Vijay Kumar Roy

Women's Movement heralded an awakening in women for their rights and brought up a feministic outlook in them. The Movement began in the West and came to India as a by-product. Aphra Ben, Mary Astell, Mary Wollstonecraft, Elizabeth Cady Stanton, Margaret Fuller, Lucretia Mott, Simone de Beauvoir, Betty Friedan, Kate Millett are some of the eminent feminists who influenced women of all cultures and races.

Women's struggle for recognition and social and political rights can be traced to Mary Wollstonecraft's *A Vindication of the Rights of Woman* (1792), John Stuart Mill's *The Subjection of Woman* (1869), Margaret Fuller's *Woman in the Nineteenth Century* (1845), Kate Millett's *Sexual Politics* and Mary Ellman's *Thinking About Women* (1968). Virginia Woolf in her essays has also raised several issues on women's cultural, economic and educational rights. Simone de Beauvoir's *The Second Sex* (1949) is considered a feminist classic that deals with 'the cultural identification of women'.

Indian English Literature came under the impact of the Women's Liberation Movement of the 1960s, a second wave of feminism. Though fiction appeared late on the scene of Indian English Literature, women appeared on it early. The advent of Toru Dutt (1856-77) on the literary scene authenticated both poetry and fiction. Her unfinished novel, *Bianca* or *The Young Spanish Maiden* appeared in 1878. The other three early novels appeared in the same decade by two women novelists - Krupabai Satthianadhan's *Kamala, A Story of Hindu Life* (1895) and *Saguna: A Story of Native Christian Life* (1895), and Sherantibai M. Nikambe's *Ratnabai: A Sketch of a Bombay High Caste Hindu Young Wife* (1895). Though we don't find the feministic outlook in these early novels, there is abundance of it in the novels of the later generation. We find women's search for identity, equality, emancipation and East-West conflict in the novels of Kamala Markandaya, Ruth Prawer Jhabvala, Anita Desai, Nayantara Sahgal, Shashi Deshpande, Arundhati Roy, Manju Kapur, Shobha De, Anita Nair, Kiran Desai and some other women novelists of the younger generation. We find their self experiences of true liberation - social, cultural, educational, legal, economic and so on.

Kamala Markandaya has many novels to her credit. Some of her celebrated novels are: *Nectar in a Sieve* (1954), *Some Inner Fury* (1955), *A Silence of Desire* (1960), *A Handful of Rice* (1966), *Possession* (1963), *The Coffer Dams* (1969), *The Nowhere Man* (1972), *Two Virgins* (1973), *The Golden Honeycomb* (1977) and *Pleasure City* (1982).

Kamala Markandaya's novels deal with the problems of women in Indian society. Her early novels have traditional notes but later she reflects upon the roles of women and their struggle for emancipation. K. R. Srinivasa Iyenger compares her works with those of Venkataramanani's. He writes that "Where Venkataramanani is poetical and masculine, Markandaya is suggestive and feminine". (*Indian Writing in English,* 439) Her first novel *Nectar in a Sieve* (1954) is a novel of shock, suffering and sacrifice. The novelist presents all these through Rukmani, the chief character of the novel, and her daughter Irawaddy. The journey of Rukmani's life is much troublesome and it reaches its climax when she is abandoned by her husband and leads a life of misery. Though at the end life changes and fortune favours her. Iyenger's remark is very apt: "One must hope and one must persevere even if one is engaged only in trying to discover 'nectar in a sieve"'. (439) Markandaya's second novel *Some Inner Fury* (1955) is a tragic novel. Though Mira, the heroine of the novel recollects her tranquility, but the suffocating death of Premala, a loving character, makes it tragic. The death of Kit and suffering of Richard make the novel more tragic. "*Some Inner Fury* is a tragedy engineered by politics, even as *Nectar in a Sieve* is a tragedy engineered by economics; and in both novels the chief characters transcend the bludgeonings of economic or political mischance and assert the unconquerable spirit of humanity." (Iyenger, 440) Her third novel, *A Silence of Desire* (1960) has the theme of faith and spiritual qualm. It presents a real picture of village people, particularly women who have faith in 'Swami' and go to him for cure of illness. Her fourth novel, *Possession* (1963) is an extention of *A Silence of Desire*. But the maturity and modernity in its characters make it different from the former. Her fifth novel, *A Handful of Rice* appeared in 1966. It has an urban setting where Ravi dreams of a respectable life and marries Nalini, the daughter of a poor tailor. But Nalini and Ravi are unable to lead their life purposefully because of the polluted environment. Markandaya's sixth novel, *The Coffer Dams* (1969) has a story of the Indo-British confrontation. Written in a new style it has an artistic flavour. Her other novels, *The Nowhere Man* (1972), *The Two Virgins* (1973), *The Golden Honeycomb* (1977) deal with 'shadowy character' of Mrs Pickering, miserable condition of Lalitha and Saroja, and love of a slum girl respectively.

Ruth Prawer Jhabvala (1927) is also a prominent figure among Indian women novelists. She has produced a number of novels which deal with the problems of Indian women. Her novels include: *To Whom She Will* (1955), *The Nature of Passion* (1956), *Esmond in India* (1958), *The Householder* (1960), *Get Ready for Battle* (1962), *A Backward*

Place (1965), *Heat and Dust* (1975), *A New Dominion* (1973) and *Three Continents* (1987). Jhabvala's novels have the themes of western culture and Indian culture. Her novels reflect the scenes of Indian women who are influenced by western culture and struggle for cultural identity.

Anita Desai (1937), a very famous name in Indian English literature attained immense popularity because of creating real pictures of Indian women. Her projection of women characters is life like. She does not rest on revealing the feelings of alienation, neglect, submission and all kinds of women's suffering in her novels, but she raises a voice against gender discrimination. Her important novels are: *Cry, the Peacock* (1963), *Voices in the City* (1965), *Bye- bye Blackbird* (1971), *Where Shall We Go This Summer?* (1975), *Fire on the Mountain* (1977), *Clear Light of Day* (1980) and *Fasting, Feasting.*

The chief women characters of her novels Maya, Monisha and Amla, Sita, Nanda and Ila Das, Vimla and Uma represent Indian women who suffer differently in a patriarchal society. The characters of her novels represent all forms of women: mother, wife, daughter, housewife, working woman, social worker and prostitute, and present their real pictures. Through these characters Anita Desai suggests that rights and freedom are attained by fighting for them.

Nayantara Sahgal (1927-) is one of the major Indian women novelists who has given a voice to women in her writings. Coming from a strong political background, she has dealt with politics in her novels. *A Time to be Happy* (1958), *This Time of Morning* (1968), *Storm in Chandigarh* (1969), *The Day in Shadow* (1971), *A Situation in New Delhi* (1977), *A Voice of Freedom* (1977) are her important novels.

Modern politics which has gone a distance away from values and ethics can easily be noticed in Sahgal's novels. Maya in *A Time to be Happy,* Rashmi and Uma in *This Time of Morning,* and Saroj and Mara in *Storm in Chandigarh* all believe in premarital and extra marital relationships. Sahgal's portrait of women characters symbolises so-called modern ambitious women who embrace and involve themselves in all kinds of activities, sometimes ignoring traditional, cultural and moral norms.

Shashi Deshpande's novels also investigate women's problems in the male-dominated Indian society. They deal with traditional and cultural values and at the same time with women's struggle for their rights, freedom and thirst for individual identity. Her important novels are: *The Dark Holds No Terrors* (1980), *Roots and Shadows* (1983), *That Long Silence* (1988), *The Binding Vine* (1993), *A Matter of Time* (1996) and *Small Remedies.* Her other two short novels are: *If I Die Today* (1982) and *Come Up and Be Dead* (1983).

Her three chief characters Saru, Indu, and Jaya of first three novels represent modern women who enjoy freedom from traditional, cultural and social restrictions. Saru, the protagonist of *The Dark Holds No Terrors* believes in inter-caste marriage and marries a man of a lower caste. She does not like the rotten tradition. She is a pure romantic and wishes to enjoy her life with full freedom. Indu, the protagonist of *Roots and Shadows* is also like Saru, a modern girl, who does not believe in casteism. She is also an example of a romantic girl who believes in love and not in social customs. Through these characters the novelist invokes in the young women the will to fight against social restrictions which come in the way of their progress and development.

Manju Kapur's prominent novels are: *Difficult Daughters* (1998), *A Married Woman* (2002) and *Home* (2006). Her *Difficult Daughters* has been tranlated into Dutch, German, Greek, Italian, Portuguese, Spanish and Marathi. Set around the times of Indian independence and partition, the novel deals with the theme of woman's struggle for existence. Virmati is the chief character of the novel who is a modern girl and marries Harish, a married professor of English. The novel explores different roles of a woman in the family and her demand for love and affection from a man. Being the eldest among eleven children, Virmati plays the role of the second mother. She looks after her brothers and sisters besides the household work but instead she is abused by her moher, Kasturi. The repeated pregnancy of her mother lays another burden on her shoulders. It reflects a bitter truth of family life and mother-daughter relationship in which daughter fails to enjoy her life hopefully and struggles for survival. Kapur's second novel, *A Married Woman,* is set around a socio-political turmoil of Ramjanmbhoomi-Babri Masjid. It is a story of an educated, upper middle class woman. It is an honest and seductive story of love, passion and attachment. The novel describes family life, sexual relationship and gender descrimination. Astha, the protagonist of the novel falls in love while in her adolescence and becomes a housewife, teacher, painter and lesbian. Her third novel, *Home* presents the life of a joint family. Nisha is a daughter of Yaspal and Sona. The novelist, through the character of Nisha describes the difficulties of a daughter who is Manglik by birth and of her parents who have to face much hindrance in search of a bridegroom.

Shobha De (1948), a true feminist, depicts the dilemma of Indian women and the erotic life of the aristocratic class. She has three important novels to her credit: *Starry Nights* (1991), *Sisters* (1992) and *Socialite Evenings* (2005).

Starry Nights is a story of a high class society. Aasha Rani is the protagonist of the novel who loves Akshay. She wants to become a film star when she is 15 years old. For this she shares bed with a film producer, Kishenbhai. Gradually the producer falls in love with Aasha but she gets engaged to Akshay, a bollywood star and sex symbol. Incidentally it comes to light that she is a pornographic actress and she does not wish to get any role in a film. Now her relations begin with an MP. A situation comes when she decides to commit suicide but she fails in it. In the end she marries a New Zealander, Jay and gets a child, Sasha. Aasha fails to realize her dream but her daughter Sasha becomes a film star. Thus the novel portrays various roles of a woman and the dark side of the film industry.

Shobha De's second novel, *Sisters* is a story of two sisters: Mallika and Alisha in which one is legitimate and another illegitimate. Their father, Hiralal, is a businessman. In this novel the novelist portrays the bad world of Mumbai. *Socialite Evenings,* her third novel is controversial. It deals with the life in the modern high society that is termed as "page 3" class where life is filled with frustration and tears. Thus her all novels depict different roles of women and the grim reality of life.

Anita Nair is a notable woman writer in Indian English Literature. Her works include: *Malabar Mind* (1997), *The Better Man* (2000), *Ladies Coupé* (2001), *Mistress* (2005), *Adventures of Nonu, the Skating Squirrel* (2006), *Living Next Door To Alise* (2007), *Magical Indian Myths* (2008), *Goodnight and God Bless* (2008) and *Lessons In Forgetting* (2010). She too, brings in light the suffering and identity crisis of Indian women in her novels.

Arundhati Roy (1961) came into literary limelight after winning the Booker Prize in 1997 for her debut novel *The God of Small Things* (1996). Kiran Desai (1971), the successor of Arundhati Roy also got international fame after winning the Man Booker Prize in 2006 and National Book Critics Circle Fiction Award in 2007 for her second novel *The Inheritance of Loss* (2006). The novel has the theme of a 17 year old girl, Sai, who lives in Kalimpong near Darjeeling and begins love affair with her mathematics teacher, Gyan, being unaware of the future consequences. Her first novel is *Hullabaloo in the Guava Orchard* which appeared in 1998.

Indian women novelists have tried to focus on the grim reality of woman's life. They delve deep into their lives and bring out all that the social order restricted since time immemorial. They have portrayed man and woman relationship that they experience in patriarchal society. The themes of confrontation between tradition and modernity and women's struggle for emancipation are the main thrust of their works. Somewhere they reflect racial conflicts and clash between Indian spiritual faith and Western materialism and then reconciliation between both to show that both are complementary to each other.

Works Cited

Beauvior, Simone de. *The Second Sex*. Harmondsworth: Penguin, 1983.

Friedan, Betty. *The Feminine Mystique*. Harmondsworth: Penguin, 1965.

Millett, Kate. *Sexual Politics*. New York: Doubleday, 1970.

Iyengar, K. R. S. *Indian Writing in English*. New Delhi: Sterling, 2010.

Naik, M. K. *A History of Indian English Literature*. New Delhi: Sahitya Academy, 2006.

Markandaya, Kamala. *Nectar in a Sieve*. New York: Signet, 1954.

—— *Some Inner Fury*. London: Putnam & Co., 1955.

—— *A Silence of Desire*. London: Putnam, 1960.

—— *Possession*. London: Putnam, 1963.

—— *The Coffer Dams*. New Delhi: Hind Pocket Books, 1969.

—— *The Nowhere Man*. (rpt.) Bombay: Orient Longman, 1975.

—— *The Two Virgins*. New Delhi: Hind Pocket Books, 1965.

Deshpande, Shashi. *The Dark Holds No Terrors*. New Delhi: Vikas, 1980.

—— *Roots and Shadows*. Hyderabad: Orient Longman, 1983.

Kapur, Manju. *Difficult Daughters*. New Delhi: Penguin, 1998.

Kapur, Manju. *Home*. New Delhi: Random House, 2006.

Roy, Arundhati. *The God of Small Things*. New Delhi: Penguin Books, 2002.

Desai, Kiran. *The Inheritance of Loss*. New Delhi: Penguin Books, 2006.

http://en.wikipedia.org

2

Woman in Indo-Anglian Literature: In Pursuit of Excellence

Ashok Kumar

There is a fascinating myth about the creation of the woman by Brahma who, in his generosity, wished to give man a companion. Since he had exhausted all the material in the creation of man, be borrowed several components from his bountiful creation, Nature, and made woman out of them. After abortive efforts on Man's part, Brahma rebuked him, "If you can not live with her, neither can you live without her". This primordial myth carries an unmistakable implication of the need for continual adjustment in man-woman relationship, indeed, that is the basis of all civilized relationships in life. Ever since the dawn of civilization, woman has been a myth and a legend, a metaphor and a symbol, a deity or a devil. But who is the real woman? What is her real entity? Has she an identity of her own? Several such questions have to be asked. About the image of woman Mary Ann Fergusson says:

> One peculiarity of the images of women throughout the history is that social stereotypes have been reinforced by archetype. Another way of putting this would be to say that in every age woman has

> been seen primarily as mother, wife, mistress, and sex object – their roles in relationship to men. (Fergusson 4-5)

India is regarded as a traditionally male-dominated society where individual rights are subordinated to group or social role expectations. In these roles, personality must not dominate the roles assigned in the societal framework. Consequently in such a set-up, a purely social, Platonic or intellectual relationship between man and woman becomes nearly impossible. A woman's individual self has very little recognition and self-effacement is her normal way of life. Indian woman too, as a part of that setup, has accepted it and lived with it for ages. Roles outside this i.e. woman as an achiever, as a leader, or as a strong individual are, by and large, either non-existent or rare. There are also exceptions but they represent the extraordinary types and not the average ones. Both male and female Indian writers have seen women in these relationships. There are deified, archetypal images and there are also debased and degraded images. Literature also portrays a few insurgent minorities who protest against the existing ills. In the ancient Indian history, by and large, women have been deified, glorified and also regarded as myths. However, in reality, most of the times, the contradictory state of affairs also existed. There was and perhaps it is there even today, a duality in the projection of the image of woman in literature. Simone de Beauvoir says:

> Much more interesting are the insurgent females who have challenged this unjust society, a literature of protest can engender sincere and powerful work. (Beauvior 718)

In Post-Independence India, when women's education had already commenced and life had started changing, the new woman started emerging. The spread of education inculcated a sense of individuality among women and aroused an interest in their rights. Women started becoming economically independent and there was a striving for the realization of their own aspirations. The society recognized virtues, merit and talent wherever they existed and gender distinctions were not taken into account. Women could, (several books bear testimony to it) besides fulfilling their distinctive roles, also participate in several other walks of life. There was an attempt at resurrection of the high-condition of woman in our society (and the process is still ongoing) after the introduction of western education, reformist movements, promotion of women's institution, the freedom movement and so on. With India acquiring an identity of her own, doors were open for women too to acquire their own identities.

Post-independence literature in India portrays all these trends and voices the clamourings of women for a new and just way of life. Over the years, the age-old image of woman seems to be slowly blurring and gradually shading off into the new image. Now when a radical change is going on all over the country, it has become necessary for a woman to redefine her new role and determine its parameters to her self and to the society, in every walk of life and perhaps revolutionize the concept of womanhood itself. There is a view, that the concept of the new woman "is a Western import born of Western compulsions" (Narsimhaiah, 245) and also that its acceptance in India like the acceptance of several other western concepts is just aping of the West and a sign of intellectual weakness. Feminist trends appeared on the horizon and they came into conflict with the conventional moral code. In fact, a set of new paradigms related to a woman's life came into existence —tradition and modernity, self-assertion and self-effacement, economic dependence and independence and so on. These new attitudes stimulated a dialogue in the life of our country. Hiatus of this kind persists in our society even today.

It is not a transplant but the product of changes going on everywhere. "It is nothing short of a revaluation", says a sociologist and looks at the new woman "as logical evaluation of the growth of the middle class and nuclear family in the last few decades." (*India Today*, 52-61) Perhaps a number of ideas do come to us from the West and this is inevitable as long as we remain a developing country. Such a phenomenon is a global one. Much of it has also something to do with the advance of science and technology, the powerful agents of change in modern society. The new woman, however, is a compulsive emergence out of the existing Indian ethos and not just a blind imitation.

The emerging new woman is a product of the inevitable transformation taking place in our society as the country marches ahead to catch up with the rest of the world. Woman striving for an identity of her own is also not just an imitation of the west. This fact is obviously clear when we look at the issues before women in the two societies. In the west, it is now purely a question of identity and equality; in India, it is still a question of stark survival. Women in India are still caught between feudal values and style of life and the fast approaching new life. Caught between the burden of the home and the work-place, child-bearing, mothering, struggling with conventions, women first have to survive, the question of equality is a far cry.

The broadly general image of the woman in literature identifies the real status according to woman in society — as mother, wife, and daughter, in that order—in a familial setting. Outside it, she is the widow, the companion etc. In the modern times she is accepted as a professional, but when she protests against injustice and exploitation, she is grudgingly termed activist and seen as a rebel or deviant.

In the present paper attempt is made to look at both - the public view of woman as represented in literature and the private understanding of woman as an individual and also as a member of society. Here it is also traced, the path of a woman and, in recent times venturing into pre-marital and extra- marital affairs, and even lesbianism. In this stage she is sometimes defiant, sometimes plainly asserting that she is only human and not promiscuous. This is at a purely personal and private level. Raja Rao—an Indian English novelist, belonging to the first generation—recreates the fundamental and archetypal image in his novel:

> Woman is the earth, air, ether, sound, woman is the microcosm of the mind, the articulation of space, the knowing in knowledge, the woman is fire, moment, clear and rapid as the mountain stream, the woman is that which seeks against that which is sought. To Mitra, she is Varuna, to Indra, she is Agni, to Rama, she is Sita, and to Krishna she is Radha. Woman is the meaning of the word, the breath, touch, act, woman that reminds man of that which he is and reminds herself through him of that which she is. Woman is Kingdom, solitude, time, woman is growth, and the woman is death, for it is through woman that one is born, woman rules, for it is she, the Universe. (Rao 357)

Often criticized as mere verbiage, Raja Rao's description in these lines is still the embodiment of the fundamental and basic image. Woman sustains life; she is the preserver of the home and a protector of culture too. There is no dearth of idealized and glorified images of women in all literatures even today. But on the other hand, the ghastly reality also exists in all its crudeness and ghastliness. Right from it's beginning, the Indian writer in English has responded with his sensibility. His sensibility records with a dissenting voice and with a note of revulsion of the social evils relating to women. Rabindranath Tagore (1861-1941), in *The Gardener,* reveals both the male and the female points of view. Women are projected as full-blooded creatures but still full of surrender. Pandita Ramabai Saraswati, described as 'the greatest woman produced by modern India and one of the greatest Indians in all history—the one who laid the foundation for woman's liberation in India,' wrote a book on *The High Caste Hindu*

Woman in which she describes a typical arranged marriage and comments:

> When the conjugal relation is brightened by mutual love, the happy wife has nothing to complain except the absence of freedom of thought and action, but since wives have never known from the beginning what freedom is, they are well content to remain in bondage. ((Tharu & Lalithia 247)

Cornelia Sorabji (1866-1954), a single woman who went to England to study Law returned to India after her education and with a spirit of adventure and missionary zeal, she helped widows in purdah and she has recorded her experience in her autobiography *India Calling*. (Ibid. 299) The Gandhian whirlwind and the Freedom Movement catapulted Indian woman into the forefront. At this A.R. Desai writes:

> This was the unique in the history of India, the spectacle of hundreds of women taking part in political mass movement, picketing of liquor shops, marching in demonstration, courting jails, facing lathy charges and bullets. (Desai 279)

Thus, women came to the front and four walls of the home widened and broadened into the boundaries of the country. Raja Rao's *Kanthapura* (1938) is one of the most significant novels of the Freedom Movement, which reveals women as taking major roles. Although women were in the forefront but Raja Rao shows that it is not in defiance of their men. Raja Rao portrays a positive image of woman as force of harmony and survival that is effectively described at the end of the novel. In the midst of the chaos created by the police, women sit and sing. A child is born. A Brahmin child widow nurses the baby of a weaver woman and women transcend the barriers of caste. Women are shown as upholders of stability. *Kanthapura* unveiled the immense potential of Indian women. Society and the writers noted the role played by women in the freedom movement and there was a shift in the sensibility towards them.

After achieving the Freedom the image of the woman as an involved participant once again is relegated to the background. However, it is only in the post-independence period that the woman's quest for identity of her own really commenced. As the country acquired a national identity of its own, the woman's quest of her own self also followed. The spark that was triggered off by the Freedom Movement now started spreading championed by reformers like M.K. Gandhi and others. But the image of the archetypal woman still loomed large on the horizon in spite of the fast growth and development of women's education.

Sri Aurbindo (1872-1950), in his *Savitri* (1954) expounds his philosophy through the account of Savitri's life. In the process, the character of Savitri is imbued with new meaning and life. The entire legend itself is made more meaningful. Savitri is the Divine word, daughter of the sun, goddess of the supreme truth who comes down and is born to save Satyavan. Savitri, like Sita becomes the central and pivotal figure of a long epic. The feminine psyche disturbed in a period of transition from tradition to modernity is voiced both in poetry and fiction. Authenticity, candour, boldness, ebullience, frankness, vehement assertion and sadness—these are some of the qualities associated with the new image.

R.K. Narayan has portrayed a wide range of women characters—from conventional to the rebellions. The conventional women dominate and are shown as supporters of the institution of family. By and large he has projected that the rebellion ends in a defeat of one type or the other. In *The Dark Room,* he has portrayed the pulls of tradition and modernity. Savitri's defiance and struggle for dignity is portrayed effectively. Rumani, her husband is a cruder Helmet and Savitri is a softer Nora. Coming to know of the promiscuous life of Rumani, she leaves the house after a quarrel. Her poignant words echo in Indo-Anglian Literature:

> I don't possess anything in this world. What possession can a woman call her own except her body? Every thing else that she has is her father's, her husband's or son's. (Narayan 72)

But she could not live on her own because of her own weakness and the oppressive social structure, though on her return to her home, slight changes have been effected both in herself and in her husband. R.K. Narayan, in his two novels *The Guide* and *The Painter of Signs* has portrayed the characters of Rosy and Daisy, who achieve fulfilment through their professions. Walking out of a marriage of her own choice, Rosy, the protagonist of *The Guide* develops into a full-fledged dancer with the help of Raju, the guide, only to realize at the end that her existence is circus-like and such existence wearies her. A role-model of some significance, Narayan has portrayed her as a woman with superwoman qualities and at that stage says Raju:

> She needs no man, neither Marco nor I had any place in her life, which had its own sustaining quality which she dose not understand. (Narayan 199)

Daisy, in *The Painter of Signs* too, establishes herself as a population control officer, but in the process, she dehumanizes herself and arrogates the male, indicating that the balance in society may be affected. R.K. Narayan seems to look at the emergence of the New Woman and he attempts at fulfilment from the angle of the society. Mulk Raj Anand has emerged as the spokesman of the downtrodden in his novels like *Coolie* and *Untouchable*. He also wrote for the emancipation of women. Although there is no dearth of conventional women in his novels, in his *Gauri* there is the portrayal of a defiant protagonist. Hers is the exploitation of the worst kind. Deserted by her husband, when she was expecting a child, she returns to her mother and step-father only to be sold to a rich man. When she finally returns to her husband, she is asked to prove her chastity. The parallelism with the story of Sita is unmistakable and he writes:

> For a brief moment the thought that the earth must open up to rescue her as it had opened up to receive Sita, came as an echo from some distant memory. But the ground was hard and solid under her feet and showed no sign of opening up. She waved her hand to forget Sita and thought of the road to the town. (Anand 220)

Mulk Raj Anand's Gauri is a blend of Sita and Ibsen's Nora. Gauri protests against a more ghastly exploitation and has been described as "the modern version of Sita". Modern English fiction rests not so much on the experiences and endeavors of male writers like D.H. Lawrence, Aldous Huxley as on the feminine insight of women novelists like Virginia Woolf, Jane Austen and Indo-Anglian novelists like Nayantara Sehgal and Kamla Markandaya. Twentieth century saw the shift from outer to inner sensibilities and no one can better understand a man or woman better than a feminine writer.

A number of women novelists have arrived on the literary scene and as in poetry, they have set out making new forays into the world of women. Anita Desai is one of the foremost Indo-Anglian writers of fiction and a glimpse of the traits of her personal life is evident in the inner journey of her women characters. Being born of Bengali and German parents, her use of English has been very spontaneous and expressive. In her novels, there is the world of radical female resistance against a defined concept of normality. Women are mostly failed questers. In her psychological novels, she has created the image of a suffering woman preoccupied with her inner world, her sulking frustration and the storm within – the existential predicament of a woman in a male dominated society. Through such characters, she makes a plea for a better way of living for women.

Going through the roles played by an Indian woman,

we see the reality that any fair sex, as a daughter or sister, a wife or a caretaker, married or widowed, has to suffer from the tyranny of Adam. She is always under-estimated, put to all sorts of humiliations, atrocities and never detached from the four-walls of the house and the suffocation of the kitchen. Simultaneously, a woman is also loosing everything that she was great of. All human values have become meaningless for her. The sanctities of home, which is another name of an Indian woman, is eroding fast, the chastity of character is depleting fatally.

Kamla Markandeya also has wider exploration, sociological and economic in her novels. She has portrayed a large repertoire of women in a changing Indian society. She is a writer who epitomizes the juxtaposition of various conflicts at different levels inside and outside the heart and mind of her protagonists and their solution, which has universal appeal. In her novel *Nectar in a Sieve*, Rukmini struggles in a changing village, and is shown as exploited. In *Some Inner Furry*, Sarojini Dandekar battles between tradition and modernity in contemporary India. These few examples reflect her firm grasp on depiction of relationships. Though women have distinctive advantages of being good storytellers and have a vivid imagination, yet no foundries can be drawn between the male and female writers and only the one who mingles the qualities of both can only be called a genius.

Nayantara Sahgal has emphasized in her novels on freedom and a new definition of 'the virtuous woman'. She has emphasized the need of awareness for women. In most of her novels, the heroines are aware of the injustice done to them in their marriage and they walk out of their homes. Her heroines reflect the changing social conditions. In spite of being deep-rooted in Indian culture they care and yearn for personal freedom and have their own identities. Civil liberties for women are another cause that Nayantara Sahgal's characters vociferously advocate. The curbing of liberties during emergency period of Mrs. Indira Gandhi's time has found detailed description in Sahgal's novels. Freedom for women, according to Nayantara Sahgal, implies awareness of her identity and raising the voice against injustice.

Sometimes they revolt against the exploitations of men and sometimes compromise with this social reality. And Nayantara Sahgal has portrayed women mostly from the upper strata and often a political backdrop is created. Family relationships and the personal shattering experience of divorce are woven deep into the fabric of her novels. Her women characters realize the importance of physical love as well as that of soul. *Storm in Chandigarh* and *Rich Like Us* explicitly propound her attitude to love, sex and marriage. Her 'women' consider men as privileged, exploiters and dictators and aspire for equality with men and freedom. Sonali of *Rich Like Us* symbolizes this desire.

She writes about the Herculean obstacles in their path. She has unraveled the inner world of women by applying 'the stream of consciousness' method and a narrative technique, which goes back and forth. She has focused on middle class educated women and there is a remarkably authentic and realistic portrayal. In the novels of all the women novelists, there is the same boldness and lack of inhibitions found in the poetry of women poets like Kamla Das. Shashi Despande's women wish to be architects of their own fate. Here is the authentic, poignant tale of the middle class educated women and their exploitation in a conventional male-dominated society. In *The Dark Holds No Terrors,* the protagonist is a medical doctor who finds herself brutally treated by her husband because she does much better in her profession. In her return to her father's home, the novelist narrates her earlier life-story. At the end, she decides to see her husband, but lives on her own and pursues her career but with a new awareness. Shashi Deshpande's *That Long Silence,* an award-winning novel, portrays Jaya, who is a failed writer, living a vapid kind of married life, which seems to have lost freshness. The entire novel brings out the stale married life in a middle class home. In accepting everything mutely, she thinks and resembles Sita and Draupadi. But realizes that it is useless to evoke such images and she says:

> I remember now that he had assumed I would accompany him, had taken for granted my acquiescence in the plan. So had I. Sita following her husband into exile, Savitri dragging death to reclaim her husband's travails.
>
> No, what have I to do with these mythical women? I cannot fool myself. The truth is simpler. Two bullocks yoked together— it is more comfortable to move in the same direction. To go in different directions would be painful and what animal would voluntarily choose pain. (Deshpande 11-12)

Shashi Deshpande in her novels has depicted effectively a disturbed but a brave feminine psyche in the new ethos. What is heartening is the fact that her protagonists are determined to encounter the world. Her novel *That Long Silence* also strikes a new note in the fact that Jaya does not wish to blame any one but owns up her own silence on all crucial occasions. But at the end of the novel, she decides to break that silence.

Nevertheless, Raji Narasinhan has treated in her novels the new liberated women in the contemporary society who really blossom. In her novels, *The Heart of Standing, You cannot fly, Forever free* and *The Sky Changes,* the new heroine is the nucleus. In *The Heart of Standing,* there is the image of a working girl living in a workingwomen's hostel and the life there and the predicament of working girls is described. In *Forever Free,* she portrays a married woman aspiring for self-fulfilment. She moves from one man to another but the same story is repeated and the novelist indicates that in the existing conditions she cannot get the harmony she wants.

The Sky Changes is an effective novel projecting Krishna, returning home separated from her husband and the process of her blossoming into a writer. Pitting against the famous Freudian statement, "anatomy is destiny",

Krishna asserts confidently "my body is not my jail. It is my boat. I will row to freedom in my boat." (Narsinhan 47) Rejecting her husband's renewed offers and being rejected by David who is in search of a body- woman, tired as he is, of the western articulate woman, Krishna is liberated to become a writer:

> I wanted my Shelley; I wanted my table and chair, my writing confinement, my sky and tense dialogues with my self. I did not want these as stolen pleasures, and forced wresting from an unwilling environment but as defining and inevitable expression of my own bring. (Deshpande 128)

The Sky Changes is a powerful novel of the realization and crystallization of the image of the new women. Krishna at the end says, "I am growing, I do not know into what, towards what, I don't feel the need to know." (Deshpande 141-2)

Though, Arundhati Roy's *The God of Small Things* is not written as a proclaimed feminist book, a slight serious women-centered reading of it surfaces many feminist issues like women's deprivation of property rights, of equal educational opportunities, of equal human states and many more. Women's issues—like wife beating scarcity of opportunities are many. With the women's awakening and with the assertion of their rights they have also asserted their right to their bodies. The female body has been a site for feminist struggle for autonomy.

Ammu, the heroine of *The God of Small Things*, being a child of a discordant marital relationship, she learns to disregard the Father Bear Mother Bear story at a young age. "In her version of the story, Father Bear beat Mother Bear with brass vases. Mother Bear suffered those beatings with mute resignation". (180) As a result, writes Roy:

> She (Ammu) developed a lofty sense of injustice and the mulish, reckless streak that develops in someone small who has been bullied all their lives by someone big. (182)

Her effrontery leaves every one to wonder, as she neither has such education nor exposure. In the absence of such influence what else one could say except that, "She was just that sort of animal", (180) concludes the narrator. Thus, Ammu is basically a different type of woman with a distinct awareness regarding injustice meted out to her because of her gender. She is also acutely aware of the discriminations against women in general and though unaggressive outwardly, she is bent upon creating her space.

With the coming of women's liberation and feminism, the move is towards the insurgence of woman in the face of the effort of man to curb her freedom. To think that the impact of these movements has caused a radical change in the insights of women would be a conceptual error. Certainly there has been a shift in values and women have started acknowledging themselves the co-equals of men. Though the high hopes of feminism have been washed away in the present social milieu, the relationships between man and woman have to work for her liberation without resigning herself to her destiny. Gender-equality still remains a myth.

It is the male ego that has given the woman an inferior status through the ages. Man has relegated her to a second-class citizen and when she could no longer endure the suppression, has revolted, her revolt ravaging like a tempest. And feminism is one such moment of protest. With a nostalgic fondness, the modern women ruminate over the *ardhanarishwara* concept that guarantees an equal status for women with men because the eternal male principle and the eternal female principle cannot but co-exist, they have existence only in contiguity.

But a handful of good willed people alone have not been able to build the foundation for women's emancipation. The women themselves have been coming forward and uniting in their march towards excellence, irrespective of their class, caste, creed or religion. The image of the modern woman, her quest and struggle for an excellent identity of her own is emerging in the Indian English Literature. Such a struggle needs some support structures out side the family to enable women to survive. Thus, a peep into the Indo-Anglian literature provides name of stalwarts who have stood for the cause of women's emancipation. Swami Vivekananda, Raja Ram Mohan Roy, Ishwar Chand Vidhyasagar, M.K. Gandhi and Jawaharlal Nehru etc., are just a few males worth mentioning.

Today women draw inspirations from empowered women like Indira Gandhi— the first woman Prime Minister of India, also known as the Iron-Lady; Vijaya Lakshmi Pandit— the first woman President of UN General Assembly; Sarojini Naidu —the Nightingale of India; Dr. Indira - the brain behind India's first Test Tube baby; Kiran Bedi —India's first woman IPS Officer; Kalpana Chawla —the first Indian- American woman astronaut; Suchita Kriplani —Veteran Freedom fighter and the first woman Chief Minister of U.P.; Mrs. Sushma Swaraj — a veteran politician; Meera Kumar— the first woman speaker of Lok Sabha; Meena Kumari, Ashwarya Rai, Lata Mangeshkar — the list is endless.

Thus, the treatment of women in Indo- Anglian Literature has undergone changes in keeping with the changing social image of women in India. Whether written by men or women, it today presents the woman, whose identity is absolutely different from that in the literature written during the earlier years. This is as it should be, because literature can have the breath and throb of life only when it keeps pace with changing image of the women. For the changed women implies changed society and no honest writer can afford, not to respond to this far-reaching change. Happily, most writers have been alike to this change and there lies hope for the future. The Indo-Anglian Literature reveals a chain of women liking up with each other as the country marching from tradition to modernity. In such a transitional period women have been playing important roles, as agents of change. Indo-Anglian Literature spans a rich variety of themes-from the theme of a conventional woman to that of the new woman, reflecting in the progress, the changes that have been going on in society.

Works Cited

Fergusson, Mary Ann. *Images of Women in Literature*. Boston: Houghton, Miffin, 1973.

Beauvior, Simone de. *The Second Sex*. Harmondsworth: Penguin, 1983.

Narasimhiah, C.D. *The Function of Criticism in India*. Mysore: Central Institute of Indian Languages, 1986.

India Today, July 15, 1992.

Rao, Raja. *The Serpent and The Rope*. London: John Murray, 1960.

—— *Kanthapura*. New Delhi: OUP, 1974.

Tharu, Susie and Lalithia, K. Ed. *Women Writing in India*, Vol. 1. New Delhi: OUP, 1991.

Desai, A.R. *Social Background of Indian Nationalism*. Bombay, 1948, 1976.

Dwivedi, A.N. *Sarojini Naidu and her Poetry*. New Delhi: Kitab Mahal, 1981.

Narayan, R. K. *The Dark Room*. Delhi: Orient Paperback, 1976.

—— *The Guide*. UK: Penguin (Paperback), 2006.

Anand, Mulk Raj. *Gauri*. New Delhi: Arnold, Heiveman, 1981.

Deshpande, Shashi. *That Long Silence*. New Dehi: Penguin books, 1989.

Narasinhan, Raji. *The Sky Changes*. Delhi: B.R. Publishing, 1991.

Roy, Arundhati. *The God of Small Things*. New Delhi: IndiaInk, 1997.

3

The Cultural Clashes: A Study of Kamala Markandaya's Novels

Narendra Tryambakrao Mane

As literature is a reflection of society, the writer as well as his literature is the product of it. It is also said that literauture is the product of a given milieu and individual sensibility which constitute together a cultural entity rooted in the changing traditional value system of people. The writer, as a human being, is a part and parcel of the society and so, naturally he gets influenced by the atmosphere around him. Therefore the literature coming out through him becomes the manifestation of the cultural, social, spiritual, political and so on scenario in the society.

Literature coming from bilingual cultures shows the tension or interaction between different cultures, languages and systems. Fiction, being the most effective and impressive form of literary exprerssion, undoubtedly occupies a significant place in Indian Literature in English. It can be said that fiction is a cross cultural phenomenon. It is the result of meeting of the two cultures. Therefore, we see in the cultural contacts two sets of values coming into conflict with each other. The majority of the Indian English writers have tried to project the tension between the two cultures. The theme of the cultural clashes has taken various forms. It has created the problem of identity also.

Kamala Markandaya, one of the major Indian English novelists, has projected the theme of cultural clashes in various dimensions. She has so many novels to her credit where her major novels deal with the cultural clashes. She delineates graphically the tensions and conflict between the people of two diverse races and two indifferent attitudes of life from various perspectives by bringing them together in different relationships and situations. Her contribution as a novelist lies essentially in her capacity to explore these vital formative areas of individual consciousness that project the images of cultural change. Some of the prominent concerns of her works revolve round the East-West encounter, confrontation between tradition and modernity and the clash of values which is closely connected to the theme of poverty, hunger, wide-spread social evils, tensions between urban and rural life, between foreign culture and native culture, between upper middle classes and lower classes of people in India. This presentation of cultural conflicts is characterised by her first hand experience. Her acquaintance with Indian life is as authentic as her understanding of the Englishmen and their character.

Markandaya's affiliation with England is a possible source of the East-West theme which is recurrent in her novels, first hinted at in *Nectar in a Sieve*, in the relationship between Rukmani and Dr. Kenny and fully explored in *The Nowhere Man* and partly in *Some Inner Fury* and *Possession*. The theme of East-West confrontation, race antagonism and the problem of expatriates are natural preoccupations for a woman novelist who being an Indian, married an Englishman. Uma Parmeswaran has rightly said about her fiction, "Kamala Markandaya's themes are not new but this weakness becomes a strength because the Indian setting still has the attraction of novelty for the western readers, and universal themes set against an

Indian background are welcome." (Quoted by RA Singh 40) Kamala Markandaya is also pre-occupied with the problems of tragic encounter between the traditional Indian values and cultural practices on the one hand, and the industrial and urban outlook on the other. The cultural encounter is presented in different levels viz. the political, the social, the human, the technological, the cultural and the artistic. Let us go through her novels to reach to the cultural clashes.

In her very first novel *Nectar in a Sieve* Markandaya strikes hard at the British industrialists, who exploit the villagers and disrupt the traditional ways of life. The story of this novel is narrated by Rukmani, the wife of tenant peasant, Nathan. Rukmani and Nathan symbolize the East whereas the rapid industrialization in the form of tannery represents the West. The tannery is built by the English people. It stands for western external forces which becomes the source of tragedy. The advent of tannery and the townsmen disturb the placid rhythm of rural existence. In this context Srinivas Iyenger writes, "...village where life has apparently not changed for a thousand years. Now industry and modern technology invade the village in the shape of a tannery, and from this impact sinister consequences issue". (438) Industry brings in the urban values and all the din and noise, filth and immorality in the peaceful village. Rukmani is aware of it. She says,

> They invaded our village with clatter and din, had taken from us the maidan where our children played and had made the bazar prices too high for us. (*Nectar in a Sieve* 27-28)

Rukmani and Nathan are representatives of the thousands of uprooted peasants under the industrial economy. The encroachment of industry causes the havoc in village economy, uproots a tenant-farmer and brings in social degradation and the loss of traditional and human values.

Rukmani is not against this modern phenomenon, but

she is against the resulting loss of values. She (Rukmani) stands for tradition while the tannery stands for modernity which crushes the culture of the village. Rukmani has to suffer lot at the hands of tannery and modernity. Her two sons die of stavation. Her four sons are lost in city culture. Her daughter, Ira, turns to prostitution to save her brother Kuti. Ira is exploited by the tannery persons. Nathan also dies. Thus, she becomes the victim of change. Markandaya's concern is with the traditional life of an Indian village in transition. S. Z. Abidi remarks, "The agrarian rural society gives way to industrial society with the resultant social values and the new social forces rising up in the villages". (103) In this novel, the presence of Dr. Kenny makes possible a slight and sketchy treatment of cultural clashes. Dr. Kenny is a good character, a humanist and representative of the finer tradition of the west. He is shown helping the poor villagers and providing them medical treatment. He helps Rukmani also. He does not like the passive acceptance by the villagers. While talking to Rukmani he expresses that:

> You must cry out if you want help. It is no use whatsoever to suffer in silence. Who will succor the drowning man if he does not clamour for his life? (*Nectar in a Sieve* 113)

Dr. Kenny does not like the Indian philosophy of fasting for the purification of soul. When Rukmani tells him about the Indian priests fasting and inflicting on themselves severe punishment, he exclaims with disgust: "My God! I do not understand you. I never will. Go, before I too am entangled in your philosophy." (114)

Here Markandaya points out that the people of East are passive and submissive whereas the people of the West are conscious of their rights. However, she speaks about the strong points of the culture of the East. In the East marriage is a sacrament whereas in the West, marriage is simply a contract. Dr.Kenny tells Rukmani: "My wife has left me. My Sons have been taught to forget me". (108)

Thus, the clash between tradition and modernity, the rural and urban, the East and West is artistically assimilated in the plot of the novel, in its characterization and atmosphere.

Her second novel *Some Inner Fury* highlights two important aspects of India's confrontation with Britain, arising out of its political dominance. This novel has a political theme which deals with India's national movement for freedom. It depicts the pre-independence Indian society in which freedom loving Indians had launched a struggle to overthrow foreign rule in the country. The novel does not depict the lives of the majority of the people experiencing injustice and oppression under the foreign rule. Like *Nectar in a Sieve,* it is a first person narrative. Mira is the narrator woman who belongs to an affluent Indian family and she falls passionately in love with an English Government official, Richard. Their love is a deep and maturing experience for both young people. But, this love is shipwrecked on the rocks of Indian nationalism entering a violent stage during the Second World War.

Different attitudes to the western way of life and the British relations with India find expression in the characters of Govind, Kitsamy and Roshan. Govind is a firy young indian who has deep hatred for the British rulers. He is the adopted brother of Kitsamy and Mira. He is a fanatic in his love for his country and holds everything in contempt. His attitude to the western influence is well expressed in the following lines:

> Govind was not and had never been a part of it. To him, it was the produce of a culture which was not his own... and alien race twisted in the process of transplantation from its home- land, and so divorced from the people of the country as to be no longer real. For those who participated in it he has a savage harsh contempt. (*Some Inner Fury* 121)

Govind also defies English missionaries, who are engaged in selfless service of the poor masses:

> To him missionaries were not merely men who assaulted the religion which was his, though he might not cherish it, impunging its austere dignities in a hundred ways, they were also whitemen, who not only set up their alien and unwanted institutions sided with those other whitemen who ruled the country, and with whom otherwise they had little in common. (142)

He is even ready to use conspiracy, violence and bloodshed against the English rulers. He burns Hickey's hospital to burn him alive. Kit's wife Premala has strong abiding to her national feelings. As a result, she has respect for revolutionary people like Govind. As she has been suffocated in the anglicized Kit's house, she often used to go to Hickey to help him in his humanitarian work. Kit's Western approach has made him alien in his own country. We can see here the clash of culture between traditional wife and westernized husband.

Though there is deep love for each other, the consciousness of national feeling separates Mira and Richard. Mira plainly rejects Richards in the courtroom during the trial of Govind. Mira remarks:

> Go? Leave the man I loved to go with these people? What did they mean to me, what could they mean, more than the man I loved? They were my poeple-those others were his. Did it mean something then all this 'young people' and 'my people'? For us there was no other way, the forces that pulled us apart were too strong. (243)

In *A Silence of Desire* we can not see direct confrontation between Indians and the British. There is cultural clash between Indian spiritual faith and the western modernism. The story of this novel moves round Dandekar and Sarojini. They are husband and wife. Sarojini is a traditional Indian housewife while Dandekar is a man of modern outlook having suspicious nature. The crisis begins when Dandekar, a government servant, suspects his wife of deceiving him by going to a Swamy for the cure of her tumour from him. Dandekar advises her to go for operation of the tumour. Surgical operation of the tumour stands for scientific cure. On the contrary, Sarojini has strong belief of getting cure with Swamy's blessings. This brings an emotional tussle between them. She retorts Dandekar when he suspects her faith:

> Yes, you can call it healing by faith, or healing by the grace of God, if you understand what that means. But I do not expect you to understand you with your western notions, your superior talk of ignorance and superstition when all it means as that you don't know what lies beyond reason and you prefer not to find out. (*A Silence of Desire* 63)

In the end, Sarojini gets ready to go for operation because the Swamy permits her:

> I am not afraid now of knives or doctors, or what they may do.
>
> All will be well. He said so. (144)

Modern education, under the impact of Britishers, makes Dandekar modern and suspicious by nature. But Sarojini's strong faith in spiritual power shatters his philosophy of life. This familial tussle is resolved at the end, but it shows the conflict between reason and faith, modernity and tradition.

Her another novel, *Possession,* puts forth the conflict between Indian spiritualism and western materialism. Valmiki, the rustic Indian artist, is the symbol of the raw independent India. Caroline Bell makes an all out effort to possess him. The conflict between the Swamy and Caroline for the custody and control of Valmiki becomes the cultural clash. It is the clash between Indian spiritual values and western materialistic civilization. Caroline Bell is a rich, devorced English lady. She is well-born and has beautiful looks. She takes Valmiki to London to develop in him the artistic talent under the influence of advanced western civilization. When she fails to get on well with Valmiki, she describes it as 'an old ailment, that England and India never did understand one another'. In her own case, her assessment is not wrong, for she fails to understand the significance of both the spiritual values of India as well as the religious motive behind Valmiki's art. Her western culture makes it diffucult for her to understand Valmiki's identification with India.

Her western aggressiveness miscalculates the real mettle of Val when she separates him first from Ellie and then from Annabel. The liberality, honesty and simplicity of Val never change. He is greatly disturbed when he comes to know that Caroline is deceiving him by sending forged letters in the name of the Swamy. Inspite of the powerful influence of the west, Val is never able to alienate himself from his Indian roots. The culture of the two countries, India and Britain, clashes when Caroline thinks that Valmiki belongs to her. Anusaya rightly observes:

> Caroline thinks Valmiki belongs to her and in a way she is right she won't let it go. People don't easily give up what they think are their possession. English never have.... (*Possession* 198)

In another novel *The Coffer Dams* the conflict is projected in the form of hostility between sophisticated British technicians and the hill-tribesmen of India. It can be said that this novel is an ambitious work of Markandaya breaking a new ground. The cultural conflict projected here starts with the construction of dam across a wild river in the South Indian High lands. This dam is being constructed by the Englishmen Clinton and Hackendrick and completed before the onset of the monsoon. Tensions are mounting up. The tribes have been dislodged from the site of the dam and they worship the river as a veritable God. Helen, wife of Clinton, takes interest in the native aborigins who were dislodged from their territory and keeps sympathy with them. Krishnan, an Indian engineer working there, tries to create upheaval by his political affiliation. Bashiam, one of the natives, who has some training was also working there. Helen takes a lively interest in him. As this project is being constructed by the English man on the land of India, naturally the conflict between two cultures occurs. While working together on the same project, British and Indian technicians remain hostile to each other and are unable to appreciate the opposite's point of view. Krishnan, the Indian engineer, disagrees with Clinton and feels bitterly hurt:

> Brush us off like flies, he thought, hurt and insult like splinters under his skin, despise us because they are experts and we are just beginning. Beginners, he repeated bitterly barred from knowledge and power as from the secrets of a master guild; and the memory of those neglectful years lay in deep accusing pools in his mind. But it's over now, he said to himself. Our day is coming. The day when they will listen to us. (*The Coffer Dams* 19)

The British officers look down upon the poor hill-tribesmen who were working there as labourers. Clinton considers them: "a tribe whose outstanding characteristic in his view was the severe retardation of its civilization." (35) While working together, whenever anything goes wrong with the project or whenever English officers and their wives face any inconvenience, they blame India and its people. In trasnsporting the crane to the site Mr. Rawling remarks: "slaving away at a thankless job in a thankless bloody country". (87)

But of all the Englishmen, Mackendrick alone is able to understand the changed attitude of Indians in the post-independence period. He feels:

> ...that the days of ostentation were over-gone with

> their proponents, the British, and their lesser copyists, the maharajas, It was the day of the common man, and the common man was done with flummery...who adopted the panoply and pomp of an English archbishop would find himself heartily jeered in any Indian town. (62)

Kamala Markandaya feels that the East and West can not come together because of inherent difference and conflict in their outlooks towards each other and she blames the West for this. Through the character of Helen this view of Markandaya is expressed as:

> Our world. The one in which I live. Things are battered down in it. Under concrete and mortar, all sorts of things. The land. Our instincts. The people who work in our factories, they've forgotten what fresh air is like. Our animals-we could learn from them, but we're christians you know, an arrogant people, so we deprive them of their rights. (138)

The novel *The Nowhere Man* depicts the encounter of an Indian immigrant in England with racialism which is savagely displayed in the English community. The conflict has been projected on the human as well as cultural level. The novelist has tried to project the gap between the Eastern and the Western cultural values. Srinivas, the central figure in the novel, is an old man nearing seventy, who leaves India and spends nearly two third of his life in England. He takes England as his own country: "This is my country now. My country: I feel at home in it. More so than I would in my own". (*The Nowhere Man 61*) A day comes when his neighbour tells him that he has no right to live in his country. When Srinivas replies he is English by adoption, he is assaulted by his neighbour, Fred. He gets a stunning blow. He realises that if he leaves England he has 'nowhere' to go:

> Nowhere, he said to himself, and he scanned to

> pale anxious eyes which were regarding him for reasons that might drive him out, a nowhere man looking for a nowhere city. (174)

He finds himself an unwanted man and tells Mrs. Pickering:

> It is time when one is made to feel unwanted, and liable, as a leper, to be obtracized further, perhaps beyond the limit one can reasonable expect of oneself. (202)

Srinivas is assured and reassured by his friends sympathetically, but racial prejudice brings him loneliness, alienation, adjustment and belonging. He says out of frustration,"I am stranger: I have been transformed into a stranger, said the unwanted man and examined a pair of hands whose stigmata would be the excuse". (241)

Markandaya has projected the racial conflict in England very effectively and with an authentic touch. Srinivas's feelings stand for the feelings of thousands of Indians and other Asians living in England who are the victims of racial conflicts and who are forced to think like Srinivas as:

> The people will not allow it. It was my mistake to imagine. They will not except physically, which is indisputable. I am to be driven outside, which is the way they want it. An outsider in England. An actual fact I am of course, an Indian. (242-43)

As Srinivas has become the victim of racial conflict in England, he once again feels alien in England, his own country of adoption. But, he has no way to go and ultimately reconciles with the situation and to his lot.

Thus, this analysis of cultural clashes shows that the Indian culture and the alien culture are the two standpoints which will never meet together. This study shows that the two cultures, two races and two viewpoints will never come closer. Markandaya herself setteled in England and experienced the wide gap between the two cultures. However, she likes them to be complementary to each other. That is why she has somewhere tried to project the reconciliation of the two cultures in her novels.

Works Cited

Markandaya, Kamala. *Nectar in a Sieve*. New York: Signet Books, 1954.

____________. *Some Inner Fury*. London: Putnam & Co., 1955.

____________. *A Silence of Desire*. London: Putnam & Co.,1960.

____________. *Possession*. London: Putnam & Co.,1963.

____________. *The Coffer Dams*. Delhi: Hind Pocket Books, 1969.

____________. *The Nowhere Man*. (rpt.) Bombay: Orient Longman, 1975.

Singh, R.A. (ed) *The Novels of Kamala Markandaya*. Bareilly: Prakash Book Depot, 2005

Iyengar, K.R.S. *Indian Writing in English*. New Delhi: Sterling Publishers, 2010.

Abidi, S.Z.H. *Kamala Markandaya : A Critical study of Nectar in a Sieve*. Bareilly: Prakash Book Depot, 2006.

4

Present Status of Women as Reflected in the Major Novels of Anita Desai

Nirmal Sharma

There are several Indian novelists who produced novels that revealed the truth of Indian societies and how women are being treated here. The struggle of Indian women for their true identity clearly emerges in the Indian English novels.

Anita Desai has enormously contributed to the growth of Indian fiction in English by incorporating Psychic aspect of her female characters who have suffered privations and humiliations, neglect and silence, aloofness and alienation. She has chosen the problems and issues faced by the women in today's male dominated world as the main theme of her novels. She presents the image of a suffering woman preoccupied with her inner world, her sulking frustration and the storm within. Through such characters, she makes a plea for a better way of life for women. She delves deep into the psyche of her women characters where she finds them struggling to strike a balance between self and society. In one of her interviews (*Replies to the*

Questionnaire) Anita Desai stated that her endeavour was to discover the significance of reality by:

> Plunging below the surface and plumbing the depths, then illuminating those depths till they become a more lucid, brilliant and explicable reflection of the visible world. (83)

The novels of Anita Desai are basically female-oriented. She probes into their problems, be it of a mother, a daughter, a sister or a wife. She writes of pure housewives, working women, social workers, and prostitutes, on the one hand and mothers, sisters, daughters, aunts on the other hand. She presents almost all types of fair sex. There is a common factor existent in all of them: all suffer from a sense of alienation whether within the family or outside it. She writes of the woman as a victim in a patriarchal, and father- dominated Indian family. The Indian woman is, forever, dominated by and dependent upon a male member of her family - be it a father, the brother, the husband, or the son. These are the various phases of an Indian woman's life and the novelist sharply focuses upon the emotional reactions of the woman as she experiences these stages. Shantha Krishnaswamy has rightly pointed out that:

> Anita Desai's novels constitute together the documentation, through fiction, of radical female resistance against a patriarchally defined concept of normality. She finds the links between female duality, myth and psychosis intriguing; each heroine is seen as searching for finding and absorbing or annihilating the double, who represents the socially impermissible aspects of her feminity. (237)

Anita Desai depicts the Indian woman as a fighter, a victim, a heroine and ultimately a winner because of her indomitable spirit and attitude of compromise. She has portrayed both kinds of women- those who are symbols of growth and change; those who are symbols of powerful means of withdrawal, regression, decay death and destruction. A woman is a giver of life, a means of moving forward and perpetuating the human race, at the same time the cruel on-slaughters of fate lead to her despondency withdrawal.

Anita Desai designs the exploration of the disturbed psyche of the Indian woman laying emphasis on the factors of loneliness and alienation. Women are suddenly confronted with the enigma of survival. However, the women in her novels do not give up the strife so easily. They indulge in self- analysis, self- discovery and ultimately compromise with the situation to live life stoically and becoming assets to the family developing the power of substance. True enough, some women characters prefer to remain in the world of illusion while many others endeavour to find a way out. In most of her novels, Anita Desai presents the psyche of a woman struggling for identity in a male-dominated universe where she is expected to amalgamate the various roles of mother, harlot, companion, and also like a sacrificial goat.

In her first novel *Cry, the Peacock,* Anita Desai portrays the lonely life of Maya whose husband Gautama wants his wife to be traditional, submissive, patient, tolerant, compromising and undemanding. In the initial years of marriage Maya tries her level best to be a duty conscious Indian wife living up to the expectations of her husband. But when she finds that her physical and emotional needs are left unattended, she becomes an easy prey to solitude and silence. Gautama often loses his patience and calls her a 'neurotic', 'mad woman':

> Showing how little he knows of my misery, or how to comfort me. But then, he knew that concerned me. Giving me an opal ring to wear on my finger, he did not notice the translucent skin beneath, the blue flashing veins that ran under and out of the bridge of gold (emphasis added)... telling me to go to sleep while he worked at his papers, he did

> not give another thought to me .... It is that my loneliness in this house . (9)

Maya's tragedy is mainly caused by her loneliness, lack of proper response from her husband, non-reciprocation of feeling between the husband and wife, her childlessness and her hypersensitivity. She dreads that she would lose her mental balance and when she is so much lost in herself without moving for a long time. Gautama says: "still sitting there? You have not stirred out? Haven't lifted up a book, your sewing? Nothing at all? But this is madness, Maya." Madness?" I screamed, leaping up at him, to strike him, to stab him... and began to cry hysterically. (178)

One day both Gautama and Maya are on the roof after a dust - storm and rain. Maya admires the beauty of the moon. When all of a sudden Gautama blocks the sight, Maya pushes him over the parapet resulting in Gautama's death. Initially, Maya is relieved. She will live a better life without Gautama, but soon she is gripped with a guilty conscience which destroys her peace of mind. Consequently, she meets with her own violent death. Maya's cry may well be the cry of an agonized woman, who suffers the pangs of loneliness.

Monisha, in *Voices in the City* is in many ways quite like Maya. After leading a stifling life in crowd of Calcutta she hopes for a freer life in Kalimpong and Darjeeling. Monisha feels stifled in the joint family of Jiban, her husband, finding the loss of privacy, of intellectual freedom, of conscience of ethics unbearable. Being aware of the plight of Bengali women she says:

> I think of generations of Bengali women hidden behind the barred windows of half dark rooms, spending centuries in washing clothes, kneading dough and murmuring aloud verses from the Bhagvad Gita and the Ramayana, in the dim light of sooty lamps. Lives spent in waiting for nothing, waiting on men, self- centred and indifferent and

> hungry and demanding and critical, waiting for death and dying misunderstood, always behind bars, those terrifying black bars that shut us in, in the old houses, in the old city. (120)

In *Where Shall We Go This Summer,* Sita, a middle aged woman, experiences a period of utter boredom and meaningless existence. She was deprived of a mother as a child while her father had no time for her. After marriage her disintegrated personality fails to recoup and casts its shadows on her relationship with her husband and children. The powerful conflict within Sita between the life- denying and the life- affirming impulses continues for a while. At last, she makes compromise with Raman. Bidulata Choudhary has summed up this situation very aptly:

> Between two uncompromising attitudes of Maya's madness and Monisha's suicide, Sita is the only heroine of Mrs. Desai to understand and succumb to the word 'only connect',... her reaction proves that it is very difficult for a woman, however, modern she may be, to get rid of the situation she is once placed in. In spite of her dislike to the ways of the world, to the traditional life of royalty, she resumes her return journey to adjust to the role of a wife and mother. Hence, she accepts defeat, crumples her passion and mingles with the prose of life for the betterment of human relationship. (77)

In *Fasting, Feasting* Anita Desai vociferously articulates the gender discrimination prevalent in society. She has also tried to unravel the psyche of the victim of gender discrimination. The novel is a powerful representation of patriarchal society governed by its dual value system. The characters, here, represent the society where daughters and sisters are married and forgotten without even the least care of their future. It is that sickening society where the birth of a son is associated with pride and felicity and considered a great boon while daughters are treated as lifelong burden. Uma, in *Fasting, Feasting,* a simple, divorced girl, becomes the victim of social cruelty due to conventional and overbearing attitude of her parents.

Though there are two grown up daughters Uma and Aruna in the family yet Papa' s desire to have a son is almost irresistible and through him Anita Desai mocks at the Indian mentality to give undue importance to sons: " Would any man give up the chance of a son?" (16) Throughout their life both of the daughters have perceived totally different behaviour of their father. But on the birth of their brother, the reaction of overwhelming father pricks their conscience-"Papa, in his elation, leaping over three chairs in the hall, one after the other, like a boy playing leap frog, his arms flung up in the air and his hair flying. A boy! He screamed a bo-oy! Arun, Arun at last!" (17)

This vulgar display of joy at the birth of son reflects typical attitude of a male member in a patriarchal society. The jubilant call of the father 'A boy... A bo-y! Arun', indicates clearly that the daughters are unwanted. From the very beginning, he aspires for a male child. Alter the birth of her brother, Uma has to assist her mother in rearing Arun. Her failure in examination provides an excuse to her parents and they withdraw her from the school without even the least care of her future. The sarcastic comments of her mother reveal her attitude regarding the future of her girl child, Uma. She says, "What is the use of going back to school if you keep failing, Uma? ... You will be happier at home. You are a big girl now. We are trying to arrange a marriage for you... Till then, you can help me look after Arun. And learn to run the house." (22) Uma's mother can still be excused for neglecting her daughter's study but her father, an educated person and a barrister, never makes an effort to educate his daughter. Ultimately, Uma gets married and immediately after her marriage, she confronts reality and comes to know that her husband is already married and he needs money to improve the deteriorated condition of his pharmaceutical factory and that makes him marry Uma. Such incidents in the life of Uma expose the gruesome reality of patriarchal system and the negligent attitude of her parents towards her future.

Another victim of patriarchal system is Anamika who is sacrificed at the alter of marriage where she is simply regarded as an interloper and is ill-treated by her in- laws. After twenty years of marriage ultimately she is burnt to ashes but her-in laws give the form of suicide to her murder. Despite committing such a heinous crime, her in-laws are not punished because Anamika's parents do not even file an FIR against them. They console themselves by saying: "God had willed it and it was Anamika's destiny." (151) Through this novel, Anita Desai mocks at the cruel and callous attitude of parents who think that all their responsibilities are over the day their daughter is married off while the son is treated as life- long asset.

After reading the novels of Anita Desai, it may be observed that the women characters of her novels live a dual life - the inner and the outer. She delves deep into the inner psychic lives of her characters showing how external forces destroy their lives reducing them to mere puppets on the stage. Her depiction of the isolated women in her novels is to make women aware of their rights in a modern social set up. The message in her writings is clear that woman can extricate themselves out of the trauma of mental psychosis by realizing that they have the power of sustaining others. This realization gives them a lot of inner strength. In her novels, Anita Desai describes the woman not only as symbols of growth and progress but also of withdrawal, in the case of Maya, Monisha and Sita, as they represent withdrawal, even death out of frustration, where as women like Uma, Mira-masi, Sophie, etc. represent a steady compromise with life. The novelist depicts women in a male-dominated and tradition- oriented society where they learn to survive both domestic injustices as well as institutionalized tyranny. The novelist makes it clear that there is no simple, straight forward solution to the dilemma of a woman. It is the awakening of her consciousness which imparts the required strength to conquer the bastion of male domination. All her female characters are depicted to be under some kind of neurosis. Some of them give up midway, while some strive towards self- fulfillment. These women characters are not passive creatures, they do have a tendency to rebel against the whole system of social relationship. Though apparently they accept their traditional roles. They are compelled to make a choice between death and life - in -death.

Works Cited

Desai, Anita. "Replies to the Questionnaire," *Kakatiya Journal of English Studies* 3 No. 1, 1978.

Krishnaswami, Shanta. *The Women in Indian Fiction in English.* New Delhi: Ashish Publication, 1984.

Desai, Anita. *Cry the Peacock.* Delhi: Orient Paperback, 1980.

Desai, Anita. *Voices in the City.* New Delhi: Orient Paperback, 2005.

Choudhary, Bidulata. *Women and Society in the Novels of Anita Desai.* New Delhi: Creative Books, 1995.

Desai, Anita. *Fasting, Feasting.* London: Chatto and Windus, 1999.

5

Musings of Agitated Protagonists in Anita Desai's *Fire on the Mountain*

Kalpana Purohit and Sunidhi Bissa

". . . . . life is reality you see on the surface—the visible world— while literature plunges the depths below that lie hidden and need to be explored and described." (Sharma 147)

Anita Desai believed that world is an iceberg - the one tenth visible above the surface of the water and is called reality, while the nine - tenth of it is submerged under water and this is the truth. Writing, for her is an effort to discover and then to underline, and finally to convey the real significance of things.

As Anita Desai can't adequately explore and express the inner, true significance of things through the medium of language in its usual and direct form therefore she uses characters, symbols and images to evoke and suggest them. She, like D. H. Lawrence, believes that:

> great art is inevitably symbolic, consciously or unconsciously, and that a novelist generally employs symbols to portray the unconscious which

> can be comprehended and communicated through the symbol only. (2)

The term symbol is quite complex and the only way to explain it is to proceed from the quality of emotion connected with the symbol. As D. H. Lawrence states, apropos of the nature, power and creation of a symbol:

> A complex of emotional experience is a symbol. And the power of the symbol is to arouse the deep emotional self, and the dynamic self, beyond comprehension. (5)

In keeping with this concept, Anita Desai resorts to the effective employment of imagery and symbolism in *Fire on the Mountain.*

An atmosphere of solitary introspection is created with the help of symbols, images and characters. Most of Desai's novels deal with symbols and images suggesting the identification of human beings with the forces of isolation and alienation. This sense of exile and alienation is a complex issue in her novels. The novel, *Fire on the Mountain* first connects then procures, engulfs and envelops to form a personal universe for each individual, making every individual's world a psychological manifestation of the individual's mind. It arises the sense of being an outsider despite living within a milieu in which one is born and bred. As Salman Rushdie, once aptly described Desai's work as *"solitude"*, her characters as *"isolators and outsiders"* - her fiction probing *"the tensions between their desired privacy and detachment, and the powerful family and social lies that both stifle and sustain."* (Quoted by Tandon 115)

Most of her protagonists are seen as neurotic, psychotic, crazy, abnormal or eccentric bordering on insanity in the beginning but when we grasp with their psychology, we begin to see them as humans with their weaknesses and potentialities. They are, indeed, caught in the web of their own compulsions, but cannot be regarded as *"haunted protagonists"* who do not come to terms with life. When understood psychologically, we begin to visualize their ambitions, disappointments and loneliness as real. They react to their troubles with tragic intensity. By her fictional rendering of neurotic behaviour, interaction and solution, the novelist not only plums human nature but also helps us to grasp their inner reality intuitively. What psychologists and social scientists treat objectively, by abstract analysis, Anita Desai provides subjectively by her aesthetic portrayal.

The psychological intricacies of the behaviour of her protagonists, their struggle to find a meaning in life symbolize the concern of modern man with the eternal human situation which speaks of the changed perspective of Writers in depicting characters. The characters of her fictional world are victims of alienation and they form an integral part of the fiction. Seldom decorative or ornamental, they reveal a world inside, a world of the inner self. They help maintain the dominant mood of the novel throughout the succession of parts, and set up a fundamental identity between the form and the content; the space and the time. Anita Desai's art is not traditional; her personages are engaged in contemplation, not action. She creates a Character in order to tell a tale and embody her vision of life and these Characters are living individuals interested in life with its hopes, dejections, and chaotic flow. They are moved by the aesthetics of existence, whatever is beautiful and good, whatever has glory and power, is only a portion of the radiance. Majority of her characters - Maya, Monisha, Raka, Nanda - live either in illusions by retreating into fabrication and fantasy, or show their reluctance to face reality; they live in a self - imposed solitary confinement. They are questers and their joy and glory lies not in completely triumphing over their confounding situations, but in the struggles they make against the prophets of doom despair.

Anita Desai is chiefly concerned with human relationships. As a novelist, she exhibits a strong inclination towards the existentialist interpretation of the human predicament. In particular, she has won a niche by exploring the emotional world of women, bringing to light the various deeper forces at work in feminine sensibility as well as psychology. This predilection leads her to examine the psyche of her women protagonists when they are confronted with the absurdity of life. She projects a tragic vision in her novels by placing her women protagonists as individuals who find themselves forced into uncongenial environments, fighting against the odds.

Fire on the Mountain goes a step ahead in voicing the multifarious aspects of humanity and theme of alienation. The novelist skillfully displays the social, economic and human problems in the lives of the three protagonists, first, Nanda Kaul, an old lady living in isolation. Second, Raka, a small girl, haunted by a sense of futility and lastly, Ila Das, a helpless woman who was in conflict with forces that are too powerful to be encountered, resulting in her tragic death. These characters are self - conscious about the harsh reality around them and so they carry a sense of lonliness, alienation and pessimism. Anita Desai adds a new dimension by turning inward into the realities of life and plunges into the deep - depths of the human psyche to score out its mysteries and chaos in the minds of character, and this she does through the stream of consciousness device. In this device, action is presented through the minds of her characters, shifting their mental time backward and forward, this is a kind of tunneling process by which she tells the past in installments. This method delineates a character and this mode of characterization, achieves by depth what traditional method achieves by extension. The motive behind using this device is to experience a total vision of life. It provides a method of presenting character outside time and place, in the double sense that, first, it separates the presentation of consciousness from the chronological sequence of events, and second, it enables the quality of a given state of mind to be investigated so completely, by means of pursuing to their ends the remote mental association and suggestions, that we don't need to wait for time to make potential actual before we can see the whole.

In this novel all the three protagonists, through this device exhibit their wrestle with the forces working against their individual identity in society. They show their willingness to wage a war against those social forces that block their smooth existence. Mrs. Nanda Kaul, Ila Das, and Raka are the characters correspondingly analyzed for their respective search for Selves and immeasurable alienation.

Nanda Kaul, Raka and Ila Das, are embodiment of the existential predicament experienced by the individual in an non-understanding and even hostile universe. A detailed analysis of the characters of these protagonists exhibit how Anita Desai has succeeded in giving expression to her world - view through these characters and by a subtle use of imagery and symbols.

Nanda Kaul is not aware of the split in her personality caused by the desire of self to recoil from all contacts and yet attempt to reach out to the other. She vacillates between two contradictory forces: withdrawal and involvement, detachment and attachment, which Anita Desai metaphorically explains through the lines of G.M. Hopkins's poem 'Heaven - Haven':

> I have desired to go,
> Where springs not fail
> To fields where flies no
> sharp sided hail,
> And a few lilies below.
>
> And I have asked to be
> Where no storms come,
> Where the green swell is
> in the haven's dumb,
> And out of the swing to
> the sea. (Desai 58)

This signifies her desire to be away from the humdrum of mundane life, to be in a heaven of nature far from the madding crowd.

Nanda, the oldest of Anita Desai's protagonists and Raka, the youngest character discussed so far, take recourse to self destructive isolation as an alternative to their conflicts, while the older woman has a tendency to look back and regret, the younger one is terrified of past, present and future, striving to shut out the agony of experiences. Both of them offer the pattern of self - alienation of the severe kind, leading them towards neuroses. Metaphysically, they point towards the futility of human existence and the inevitability of human suffering. Raka and Nanda suggest a sickness of soul which is imposed upon them from inside. Outer forces do affect the workings of their minds, but their trouble is ingrained in the sense of insecurity developed in the claustrophobic atmosphere they live in. Nanda's difficulties arise out of her intense self - contempt generated from her dismal failure in life. Her has been an existence choked with activities - the multiple responsibilities of running a household, looking after children, and maintaining a social status of V.C. husband. In the words of Harish Raizad:

> From the musings of her agitated mind it appears that as the wife of the V.C. of Punjab University and the mother of several children, she has lived a very busy and tiring life. (44)

And after such a hectic life, with all the mundane responsibilities discharged, a wish for a quiet spell of aloneness and contemplation is understandable. But, Nanda Kaul, does not look for peace in Kasauli. She likes the emptiness of "Carignano" and enjoys the 'starkness' of the town.

The novel incorporates a 'bizarre psychology'. In her frustration, Nanda frantically searches for detachment. She wants to withdraw from the milieu and merge with the pine trees, free from all,"unwelcome intrusion and distraction" (Desai 3)

She longs for the privacy, seclusion, tranquility and solidity of trees:

> She stepped, backwards into the garden and the wind suddenly billowed up and threw the pine branches about as though to curtain her. (3)

The comparison between Nanda Kaul and her garden, drawn by Anita Desai is highly evocative:

> Like her, the garden seemed to have arrived, simply by a process of age, of withering away an elimination, at a state of elegant perfection. It was made up of a very few elements, but they were exact and germane. . . . . (19)

This symbolizes that she has become so much immune to tender emotions that she does not feel any difference between a living person and an inanimate object. Life has not honored her claims. So much is made of the protagonist's rebelliously detached attitude and her desire to live in complete isolation that we tend to regard Nanda Kaul as a formidable old woman who has snapped all ties and discarded everyone. Strongly convinced that life had dealt a raw deal to her, she treasures her freedom and her privacy. She is glad that her responsibilities towards her family are over, glad she needs nobody and nobody needs her now. "She wanted no one and nothing else. Whatever else came, or happened here, would be unwelcome intrusion and distraction."(3)

Even Raka did not bother much about the,"blatant lack of warmth"(40) exhibited by her great grandmother. But on the other hand, it is hard to believe that Nanda is basically a complaint character for whom love is the most desired sentiment, above everything else. Her 'flashbacks' of her over busy days reveal that Nanda strikes a bargain with fate which Horney terms as a 'Deal':

> Too many trays of tea would have to be made and carried to her husband's study, to her mother - in law's bedroom, to the verandah that was the

> gathering place for all, at all times of the day. Too many meals, too many dishes on the table, too much to wash up after. (29)

She is ever engaged in her duties disavowing her pride and thinking that if she is good and dutiful then others will treat her with love. But the realities of life give her a raw deal. Her husband's infidelity, his utter disregard, the callous attitude of her children give her blows. The choices are limited for Nanda - to fight it or bear it mutely. She chooses the second alternative. Also to save her from self - berating, she quickly builds around her a citadel of self glorifying virtues. Quietly, she engages herself in the discharge from her family duties.

This is the portrait of a silent sufferer, a martyr, a "sub - dued victimized self", who thinks herself as a, 'night - cat' prowling in the dark, but unconscious forces tell her that she is like the bird flying unevenly, 'through the funeral moonlight'. These images flash across her mind when her husband leaves her alone to carry on his love affair. To relieve the tension of the situation, she considers her aloneness as, "a moment of private triumph, cold and proud." (26)

But, Nanda is neither triumphant, nor proud of her aloneness. She is bitter. Only in order to hide the inner fear of isolation she creates a facade of pride and victory. If she were really proud of her life of withdrawal, she should not have wallowed in self - pity. Throughout the narrative, the refrain is, "Discharge me. . . . . I've discharged my duties. Discharge." (30) with a strong note of compunction. She derives a weird sense of happiness, of a release from bondage, when the responsibilities are over. It is to be remembered that Nanda Kaul has nothing to look forward to. Her children are alienated from her. Her misery is implicit in the last sentences she utters before her death:

> And her children - the children were alien to her nature. She neither understood nor lovedthem. She

> did not live here alone by choice - she lived here alone because that was what she was forced to do, reduced to doing. (145)

She is a forsaken woman and this dismal sense of having failed at everything in life produces self - reproach and self - contempt. In order to escape the self hate, Nanda found the easiest course, and shifted her energies from complaint drives to resignation. An atmosphere of impersonal relations suits her. She has achieved the desired loneliness and feels happy. She has, however, over - looked the basic principles that the past cannot be shut out by fleeing it. Nanda confronts her past in Ila and Raka, and is ensnared in her memories and so she bitterly resents Raka'a intrusion because it awakens past memories in her. She is one of the links of the long chain of events Nanda wishes to forget. So is Ila Das whom she avoids. Both Raka and Ila Das represent that identity which Nanda strives to forego. Her constant effort is to become anonymous, faceless to, "merge with the pine trees and mistaken for one. To be a tree, no more and no less, was all she was prepared to undertake." (4) At another time, her desire is to lie still, to,"be a charred tree trunk in the forest, a broken pillar of marble in the desert, a lizard on a stone wall."(4)

A tree trunk could not harbour irritation nor a pillar annoyance. She would imitate death like a lizard. This death wish shows that she does not want to undergo the past torture again.

Raka's arrival at Carignano does not elicit an affectionate response. No tangible bond of tenderness develops between them. Nanda Kaul views Raka as, "an uninvited mouse or cricket." (85) Stealthily entering the barren and rugged world of Carignano. She despises almost everyone who comes her way: whether be her haughty complacent daughter, Asha, her pale and fragile grand daughter, Tara, her elusive and volatile great granddaughter, Raka or her old and decrepit companion Ila Das.

It is quiet unlike the reaction one would expect from a great grand mother. No affection grows between Raka and Nanda as their solutions of withdrawal clash. Sometimes Raka excels her great grand mother in her eagerness to know all that is unknown to her. She shows certain extra ordinary traits as a child for the persuasiveness of Nanda's secret life.

"If Nanda was recluse out of vengeance for a long life of duty and obligation, her great grand daughter was a recluse by nature, by instinct. She had not arrived at this condition by long route of rejection and sacrifice -she was born to it, simply." (48)

Even Nanda acknowledges the greatness of Raka as a recluse. Anita Desai, like George Eliot, analyzes Raka for her hidden and unseen motives of life. Unlike Nanda Kaul, Raka is an explorer who dislikes a duty bound code of life: "Raka had all the jealous guarded instincts of an explorer, a discoverer." (61)

Unlike her great grand mother, she is a born explorer: she stands for the definitive purpose of life. With an eagle's eyes, she explores her existence beyond the apparent view of the readers. Like a discoverer, she analyses each and every object with a keen intensity of a scientist. She has been witness to the brutality and futility of human existence. She is haunted by the recollections of the nightmarish nights that have made her almost a child - stoic. Her childhood has hardened her into a little core of solitary self - sufficiency and now, her spirit is defiant enough to go chanting: "I don't care, I don't care, I can't care of anything." (73)

Children of her age are often attracted towards the beauties of existence: fairy tales, adventure stories, flowers, butterflies. Raka, on the contrary, relates to ugliness. She possesses a weird imagination and is drawn to uncanny places and things. She is not a normal child. Her granny's imaginatively spun stories can hold her interest only for a short while. The bizarre spots of Kasauli, the charred house and trees have an immense fascination for her. Raka's psychological alienation can be ascribed to her unfortunate home which leaves the child insecure and isolated. If the world is so much hostile, the easiest course is to withdraw from it. Instinctively, she learns to expect nothing from it. Conversely, she gives nothing to it. Raka is unable to get in touch with her impulses at the 'wish' level and is thus handicapped in finding the deeper roots of her own thrust into life.

Through Ila Das, Mrs. Desai lets the wheel of time come in full circle. Past memories of Nanda Kaul unfold the vision of time:

> My dear, you can't imagine you have no idea what it has meant to me to have you here at Carignano, to come and see you today. Why, its been a little bit of the past come alive. As if the past still existed here and I could simply come and visit and have a cup of tea with it when I was tried to the present." (132)

Ila brings forward the social cause of humanity, as a social reformer. She fights against evils like social ignorance and superstitions. Born and brought up as a Christian, she never enjoyed the status of the privileged one. Ila deliberately chooses the hard life of a social worker. She had a divided family, as all her sons had been sent to foreign universities, but none of them excelled in his discipline. Ila's husband paid all the debts, but her sons were so selfish that they did not even turn up on the death of their father. As Ila Das relinquishes all her physical and worldly attainments, she undergoes a metamorphosis of character. This change in her enables her to embrace a wider vision of life for serving the cause of humanity. She has no religion of humanity. As she fights for the women's cause, she encounters injustices, cruelties and atrocities against them in the male - dominated society:

> I do believe the women would listen to me if it weren't for that impossible priest. It's so much

> harder to teach a man anything. Nanda - the women are willing, poor dears, to try and change their dreadful lives by an effort, but do you think men will let them? Nooo, not one bit. (129)

She faces all round opposition to her reforms, but like a Karma - Yogi, she carries on her work as a social welfare officer. She never cared much of the consequences of it. One day, when she was coming back from Carignano to her home, she faces her doom, humiliation and finally death at the hands of Preet Singh, a native of the same village. The murder of Ila Das suggests the deterioration of human values. It becomes symbolic of the growth of animalism in man.

So far, Nanda manages to avoid the onslaught of self hate by escaping alternately into the intra - psychic defenses. Finally, the telephone call, announcing the death of Ila Das, overwhelms her with spite of herself. Metaphysically, the deaths of Ila and Nanda are interpreted as the final reality suggesting the futility of human existence. Ila dies because of her concern for others, Nanda dies because her concern for loneliness. Both involvement and non - involvement signify a tragic sense of unfulfillment. From psychological standpoint we analyze the forces destroying Nanda as the compulsions of self - destructive drives generated by the torment of a life which has been a failure.

On receiving the news of Ila Das's death Nanda'a self hate operates in several ways. That she fails to stand up to her glorified image impinges upon her unconscious. She is overwhelmed by the feelings of worthlessness and inadequacy. A loving individual as she is, she should have thought of asking Ila to stay on at Carignano. Self reproach proclaims her guilty, she is lowered in her self esteem. She lived in a make belief world to compensate for the cruel reality and her aggression directs against her "self" because she has to cope with the struggle between her idealized and real selves. In her last moments we discern that behind the fabricated and fragmented world reflected by her self accusations, lies the vision of reality; a belief interplay of life and death, destruction and renewal, chaos and cosmos. Finally, the negative values, chaos and destruction overpower her real self which a life time of pretences has already enfeebled. An inevitable by-product of the confrontation between real and idealized selves is inner conflict. Nanda condemns herself as a murderer of Ila. Self destructive drives work on her silently but fatally. She doesn't commit suicide but her death wish, expressed in preceding pages works on her psyche. It finally causes her psychic death, followed by a sudden physical demise.

The silent self - annihilation of Nanda is followed by a more violently destructive act of Raka i.e. setting the hill side to fire: "Down in the ravine, the flames spat and crackled around the dry gross and black smoke spiraled up over the mountain." (49) By an elaborate expression of her free will and demonstration of her ability to choose and act, she sets the forest on fire, and this fire created by her is result and manifestation of her existential angst to destroy the old and meaningless and to make room for the new and significant. It is an affirmation of her search for values in an otherwise futile existence.

The suffering of these alienated and isolated protagonists is aptly exhibited through her felicitous and deft use of symbols and images. Anita Desai uses symbolic and functional imagery and symbols as the sole ingredient of her art. Imagery and symbolism in Anita Desai may be considered to constitute the poles of an axis on which her fictional world revolves. Her symbolic world of fiction, themes of despair and socio-psychic fragmentation have been picturesquely presented through telling and tantalizing images.

There are several images and symbols that deepens the philosophic implications of the novel. Carignano, Nanda Kaul's present abode, stands for the individual self divided from within. It is the symbol of despair and desolation, which depicts a dreary, desolate and forlorn picture suggesting Nanda Kaul's isolation. It throws light on the musings of the lacerated self's immured existence, and is, metaphorically pictured through the symbols of walls, boundaries and barriers. The desolate and haunted house in Kasauli inscapes the life of Nanda. Though, she lives there under compulsion deserted by her sons and daughters after the death of her husband, yet she is content with its stark, secluded and sunny splendour. The seclusion and serenity of Carignano defines the stillness and freedom, Nanda has been able to achieve in her old age. Carignano is Nanda and Nanda Carignano.

The **Eagle** symbol is repeatedly used in the course of the novel to highlight quest. The sight of the Eagle flying high, makes Nanda long to be able to soar like the bird and this longing for soaring above the reach of deterministic confines is the hallmark of Raka's character. Thus Nanda and Raka attempt to merge in the Eagle symbol, which denoted their existential angst and quest for selves.

The **forest fire** scene has symbolic overtones. Like "The Fire Sermon" in T.S. Eliot's *The Wasteland* The fire in *Fire on the Mountain,* " . . . is a destroyer. It is also a purifier." (Brown 557)

Fire is symbolic of Raka's wild nature and also cruelty and violence in the world. Raka the invalid, restless little girl who is a product of a broken home, becomes the symbol of forest fire as she strives to find or create values and significance for her existence.

Mountain symbolizes Nanda Kaul. It can even be taken as an escape world of Mrs. Kaul where she seeks some kind of reconciliations. It acts as a psychological defense for her but when Ila Das is raped and killed this defense mechanism gets shattered. The suppressed emotional volcano explodes in the form of *Fire On The Mountain.*

The prey-predator image of **hen pecking** at a worm is suggestive of Nanda Kaul's present turmoil. Her past suffering at the hands of the adulterous husband and her present awareness about the harsh realities of life are both successfully established by this image:

"Still staring at the hen which was greedily gulping down bits of worm, she thought of her husband's face and the way he would plait his fingers across his stomach...." (Desai 22)

Recurrently employed image of the **Pine Tree** that stands burnt and alone, and is often an object of attraction for Nanda Kaul:

"She was grey, tall and thin .... She fancied she could merge with the pine tree and be mistaken for one. To be a tree, no more and no less, was prepared to undertake." (4)

This image also contributes to the existentialist theme of the novel: "Nanda's sense of identification with the pine trees suggest her desire for absolute stillness and withdrawal from life." (Indira 97)

These images and symbols of anguish in the external world of sights and sounds mature to images of spiritual identification of the inner world of the psyche. Rhythmatically condensed, subtly chiseled colour these images and symbols are knitly woven into the characters to point out the emotional chiaroscuro through successive stages of alienation leading to self-identification.

Thus, it would be apt to sum up the significance of symbols and images in *Fire on the Mountain* in the following words of a critic, S. Indira:

> "It is the charming mosaic of imagery woven so skillfully by the novelist that makes the novel a work of art. This novel deprived its imagery, would be an ugly skeleton, chilling the reader." (96)

Works Cited

Bande, Usha. *The Novels Of Anita Desai : A Study in Character and Conflict*. New Delhi: Prestige Books, 1988.

Brown, Clawin. S. *The Reader's Companion to World Literature*. New York: Penguin, 1984.

Desai, Anita. *Fire On The Mountain.* New Delhi: Allied Publishers, 1977.

Gopal, N.R. *A Critical Study Of The Novels Of Anita Desai.* New Delhi: Atlantic, 1999.

Indira, S. *Anita Desai as an artist.* New Delhi: Creative Books, 1994.

Kumar, Gajendra. & Ojha, Uday. *Indian English Literature: A Post ColonialResponses.* New Delhi: Swarup & Sons, 2005.

Raizada, Harish. *The Haunted Protagonists of Anita Desai.* Ghaziabad: Vimal Prabhakaran, 1984.

Sharma, Kajali. *Symbolism in Anita Desai's Novels.* New Delhi: Abhinav Publications, 1991.

Singh, Anita. *Existential Dimensions In The Novels Of Anita Desai.* New Delhi: Atlantic, 2001.

Tandon, Neeru. *Anita Desai & Her Fictional World.* New Delhi: Atlantic, 2008.

Tiwari, Shubha. *Critical Responses To Anita Desai.* New Delhi: Atlantic, 2004.

6

New Woman -Inching Towards Freedom: Predicament of Woman in the Novels of Shashi Deshpande

Dalvir Singh Gahlawat

Shakespeare describes woman in Hamlet as, "Frailty, thy name is woman!" (1.ii.146). According to Nietzsche, "Woman is the diversion of the hero". (Beauvoir 244) D.H. Lawrence has an entirely different view. To him she is neither a diversion nor a prey; "she is not an object confronting a subject, but a pole necessary for the existence of the pole of the opposite sign". (245)

Every man is a child of his age. He is influenced by the age, though if he is a man of letters, he may influence it also. An author belongs to his race and age; the spirit of his race and age finds expression through him. A writer is generally said to be "not of an age but of all ages". A creative thinker is by definition a socio-political being. Her or his worth lies in preparing and nurturing certain principles, which make the earth a better place to live in. Writers, therefore, cannot confine their words merely for entertainment; they need to communicate with more somber and anxious issues in the society. They are a reflection of the society. They return to the society what they receive from it. They not only reflect the various discourses of the society they live in, but also intervene to reform it as well. Therefore, they cannot escape from the spirit of their own age. Shashi Deshpande is amongst those writers who convincingly express the dialectical relationship between a culture and its art.

Indian fiction in English has been augmented by several highly talented women novelists including Kamla Markandaya, Anita Desai and Shashi Deshpande. They have written of Indian women, their conflicts and predicaments against the background of contemporary India. Women are natural story-tellers even then they do not write creatively or publish; they struggle to give form and shape to their autobiographical accounts, which attract publishers both in India and abroad.

In the context of contemporary Indian writing in English, Deshpande is one of the most understated, yet confident voices. She explores individual and universal predicaments through the female psyche. Her novels include *Roots and Shadows* (1983), *The Dark Holds No Terrors* (1980), *That Long Silence* (1988), *The Binding Vine* (1993), *A Matter of Time* (1996), and *Small Remedies* (2000), in addition to two short crime novels - *If I Die Today* (1982) and *Come Up and Be Dead* (1983) - and six volumes of short stories. Besides these, Deshpande has also written books for children.

Sahitya Academy Award winner, Shashi Deshpande occupies a prominent position among contemporary Indian novelists in English. She deals with the middle class Indian woman who represents the overwhelming majority of Indian women and is struggling to adjust in it rather than get freedom from the traditional world. She was born in 1938 in Dharwad (Karnataka), India. She is the daughter of the renowned Kannada writer and Sanskrit scholar Adya Rangachar, who wrote plays of ideas. From her father nevertheless Shashi Deshpande must have acquired an intellectual bent of mind and love for reading and scholarship, which have won for her degrees in economics, law and English and a diploma in journalism which she finished with a Gold medal. Her major concern is to depict the anguish and conflict of the modern educated Indian women caught between patriarchy and tradition on the one hand, and self-expression, individuality and independence for women on the other. Her fiction explores women's predicament to fulfill herself as a human being, independent of her traditional role as daughter, wife and mother.

Shashi Deshpande worked for a couple of months as a journalist for the magazine *Onlooker*. She started writing at that time and published her first short story in 1970. Her stories were published in magazines like *Femina, Eve's Weekly*, etc. *Legacy,* the first anthology of her short stories came out in 1978, and her first novel, *The Dark Holds No Terrors* was published in 1980. In June 1999, The Feminist Press of New York brought out her novel, *A Matter of Time,* her first work to be published in the USA, and in 2004, Penguin Publishing House, New Delhi published her latest novel *Moving On.* Till now she has published nine short story collections, ten novels (including two detective novels) and four books for children. Her works have been translated into various Indian and European languages.

Women writers' fiction constitutes a major segment in Indian English literature. They had to struggle a lot to establish their identity and to assert their individuality; it has led women to wage a desperate fight against the existing social order of the day. Shashi Deshpande's women are aware of the cultural and social shortcomings to which they are subjected in this male-dominated society. They rebel against their men in search for freedom and identity, but ultimately find themselves up against well-entrenched social inertia. Being aware of the predicament of a woman in this male-chauvinist society, they seek a change in the civilizing norms and do not want to repeat the past practice. They looked at it as an alternative to the bondage imposed by the parental family and opt for it.

Deshpande, in her fiction has described some basic issues of the power structure and role division in the patriarchal society of India. Today, women have comprehended that their inferiority is not designed in heaven but it is the creation of male-dominated society. Women are trying to unshackle themselves from subordination by defining their potentiality. They are aghast with the male notion of women's place and are redefining themselves as well as their proper place in male controlled society. They can put up with the exploitation and discrimination no more. They are trying to abolish gender discrimination prevailed in the society by revolting against sexual politics and gender requirements.

All the protagonists of Shashi Deshpande investigate the factual social and touching bonds that shackle women. The 'new woman' meets the tradition-oriented society and it is she, who has to bear the twin whips of custom and contemporaneity. The conflict between traditional values and the impact of education and employment is sufficiently described in *Roots and Shadows* and *The Dark Holds No Terrors*. A shift to the wise presentation can only be found in her novel, *A Matter of Times*. Deshpande depicts women in myriad roles—wife, mother, daughter, and above all an individual in her own right. Her concern is always with a woman's chase for her identity. She makes efforts to launch the woman as an individual, who breaks loose from the traditional constraints and moulds her identity in tune with the altered social atmosphere of modern times.

In *Come Up and Be Dead*, Kshama has a full-blown crisis on her untested and still timid hands. She is bold and has the courage to fight the situation elaborately. When she faces the incidents of murder in the school she does not discourage herself. Therefore it is said about her that:

> "there was no doubt at all that the woman who stood on the dais was fully in command both of the situation and herself. Small-made and dumpy though she was, there was as unmistakable air of authority about her. ...each hair in place, the sari hanging in geometrical straight lines from waist to feet, from shoulder to hip, in the subdued faces of the teachers and the awed silence in which the girls shuffled in. ... here's a woman who knows what she wants. And gets it" (5)

This crisis that she faces was no ordinary one. Mridula, one of the schoolgirls, is found dead. Rumor is strife. Was it suicide? Was there foul play? It is common knowledge that the girl was pregnant at that time. Accusing fingers are even pointed at Kshama's own brooding and somewhat strange brother Pratap. But before anybody has the time to sort out the situation, another tragic death, that of Pratap, comes to light which itself is soon enough obscured by the strangling death of one of the teachers. Finally the headmistress' cousin Devayani tells the story of how she confronts the murderer and gets trapped and is on the verge of being murdered too. Kshama faces all this boldly.

Devayani is a homemaker, homebound and, as far as one can tell, living her life according to the prescribed norms. However, the death of her parents forced her to find some shelter, and rather than working as an unpaid servant at her sister's place, she preferred to work as Kshama's housekeeper. She feels she has no option but to work. Towards the end of the novel, she returns to her home realizing that she could find release from this imposed imprisonment, and she begins to write the script of her life for herself. After getting a divorce, Jyoti Raman is alienated from her family as they blamed Jyoti for everything. Afterwards, she completed her education, got a job and moved away from her disapproving family along with her daughter to start a new life.

The novelist in *Roots and Shadows*, tries to express

through Indu that it is the educated and the creative woman who will liberate herself and sacrifice to women's liberation, both, enthusiastically and excellently. Indus's predicament is represented as the predicament of women in general in the existing system of Indian society going through a transition from the old to the new. Her predicament is tattered between customary and individual views. Her awareness of the sanctity of the familial bonds fetters her from the prompt action of feelings. Though these bonds appear to be unjustified in the beginning, gradually she learns to be bound by them as a typical traditional Indian woman. She knows that transgressing them will certainly break the family knots. Indu is able to get herself free from the shadows that bind her to the past, only after Akka's death. Being forced by Akka's will to do the responsibility of the family matriarch, she displays maturity and strength in executing her duties. She realizes that Jayant, her husband, need not determine or limit her sphere of activity. Indus's decision not to submit herself to anyone's dictates, not to get influenced by her husband in career matters shows that she is making independent decisions that mature her into an individual who chooses to live life in accordance with her own wishes in a bold and challenging woman of determination. She wipes out all feminine limitations and also holds the power to transform others.

Akka has to face the indifference of her husband as she represents the older generation. The older age group women have suffered sexual brutality, widowhood, drudgery etc. The patriarchy has strengthened among the working class due to the lesser opportunities of education, especially for women. Men have mistresses and they neglect the family. Women have to play the roles of breadwinners and caretakers of children and the family. Physical violence, sexual abuse and mental torture are a fact of daily life. In this novel Indu, in the end, makes resolutions to change herself through self-realization. Indu, as a journalist and a writer, writes about women; she is forced to write fabrication about a certain woman.

Thus, the 'New Woman' as Jaya, Saritha and Indu, after their marriage, realize that marriage is another enclosure that prevents a woman from her awareness as an independent human being.

The Dark Holds No Terrors reflects women's awareness. In this novel, Saru is represented as the spokesperson of middle class working women in modern India. She rebels against traditional norms but eventually tries to compromise with the existing reality. No sooner does Saru, the doctor, take great interest in her profession and in her patients than her professional success casts a dark, negative shadow on her married life. In spite of the suffering she faces the situation very courageously and thinks that escapism is never a solution, and, that she is her own refuge.

Through Saru, Deshpande tries to establish the woman as an individual, who breaks the traditional impositions and refines her identity in accordance with the changed societal atmosphere of modern times. Now she is able to have some significant control over her relationships and career. Although the women do not get womb-like security in their parental home yet they get help to raise questions, which they had never dared to ask themselves. Sarita, a medical doctor, who married a low-cued Manohar against her parent's wishes, walked out of her parental house. But, now, on the pretext of her mother's death, she goes back to her father's home, hoping to find consolation away from her husband's fearsome and enigmatic brutality. Unable to adjust to the social demands, Saru contemplates about her hidden strength and digs it up. She learns not to suppress her talents. She is capable of viewing her future more positively, only after analyzing her past ideas and attitudes. Sarita ponders:

> And to do that I must get away, yes, that's why I'm going. To get away from this house, this paradise of matching curtains and handloom bed spreads. The hell of savagery and submission? (25)

It is only when Sarita goes away from her immediate family, her husband and children, that she is able to overcome her sense of guilt. This sense of guilt has been thrust upon her by societal norms on the expectations of others. It is when her mother keeps repeating very often, that Sarita begins to hold herself responsible for her brother Dhruva's death. Much later, her father says, "I never blamed you". (10) At this point she is able to see the false accusation. She realizes that she has not failed as a daughter, but it was her mother, who had shut her out of her affections and even cursed her after Dhruva's death:

> "Why didn't you die? Why are you alive when he's dead?" Her mother continues to curse her; as - "Daughter? I don't have any daughter. I had a son and he died. Now I am childless..." (12)

Sarita now sees that she has been shut out by her mother from her world. This withdrawal helps Sarita to get rid of the guilt complex too and holding herself responsible for Manohar's sadism. She knows very well that her success at work has made Manohar a monster at night. She has will power and knows how to overcome the hurdles of her life. She attains her inner strength and tells her father to request Manohar to wait. Her withdrawal is not an escapist's but a withdrawal which is essential for her re-integration into society. She is able to break the illusions that she had created and faces life courageously.

A pleasant and personal existence within the family environment is attempted by the protagonists of Shashi Deshpande. Perhaps, that is why Shashi Deshpande is helped by the Indian culture, in moulding her protagonists. They protest for the right to be recognized as individuals. They introspect and do not go beyond in order to search for freedom. The obdurate feminine-self finally finds its roots in the home and with husband.

That Long Silence explores the feminine voice. Jaya, in this novel, though a new woman, is caught up in an orthodox trap, experiences an impulsive urge to be empowered simultaneously with a natural urge to be traditional and conservative. Jaya, apart from being a housewife, is a creative writer too. At the beginning of the novel, Deshapande's protagonists always have a certain shock; here, Jaya's husband is accused of corruption and is forced to remain in hiding for a few days. Jaya and Mohan shift temporarily to their Dadar flat. This happening compels Jaya to think. The writing of this novel *That Long Silence,* is described as:

> ...like one of those multicolored patchwork quilts that Kakis make for any new baby in the family, so many bits and pieces -a crazy conglomeration of shapes, sizes and colours put together. (*That Long Silence* 21)

Jaya, through the patchwork of her written life, realizes that she alone is responsible for both her achievements and failures. She begins to see the truth of the dictum, "Do as you desire" only after this period of withdrawal. Jaya is in a state of turmoil, when Mohan walks out of their Dadar flat. She is alone at home with her neighbours Mukta and Nanda who care for her and bring her back to normalcy out of her confusion and fear. Jaya is physically alienated from her family temporarily. The next two days, Jaya writes continuously, pouring out all that she had attempted to suppress in the past. After hours of contemplation, Jaya takes the decision to give up the role of a silent and passive partner and to clarify the misunderstandings and the turbulence in her relationship with Mohan. The novel ends with the recovery of faith. Jaya's decision to break the silence, which has distorted her interactions with her husband, may be symbolized as a new hope.

Jaya's attempt of breaking the silence represents in general all oppressed women in the male-ordained society. Hence, she sacrifices her creative writing skill to be a good wife and finds herself satisfied with writing the blameless heart under the pen name Seetha. She begins to write what people want to read and not what she wants to write. It is here, exactly, that the writer brings out the restrictions under which women writers try to express themselves. It is only in the end, she gradually begins to realize that her very compromise shatters her individuality, and has led her to be victimized. She decides that she will live without sacrificing her identity or individuality; she makes some adjustment of her own desire, taking care to see that she does not lapse into servility. Her decision to have her own way gives new confidence to her and this confidence makes Jaya face the realities of life and she decides to break her silences by speaking out.

The Binding Vine deals with women's experience of existential trauma. This novel is significant for the idea of female attachment; the desire of one woman for female bonding, and helps another, who is less fortunate. This positive development can be seen in Urmila. She strongly believes that women should have the courage to express themselves. Urmi's attempt to expose the ghastly reality of Kalpana's life is an effort to oppose a "society in which such feminist creams have been changed by basic patriarchy that separates women into rigorous categories based on function." Urmi is determined to break the silence of women which binds her in different forms -sometimes in the name of social taboos and sometimes in the name of the family honour. She justifies her stand as she observes these mishaps from the female point of view. She realizes her responsibility towards her own caste - women - and tries her best to bring its truth before the society. Urmila leaves no stone unturned in fighting, not only for her own battle, but also ventures to facilitate other women, the poor and the oppressed. She is self-reliant from the very outset and much conscious of her identity. She draws the attention of the society to the dissimilarity of sexes and feels no anguish in attempting to change the existing societal norms. In spite of all this, she does not rebel against the established system, for she believes that the things are improving gradually.

The novel shows the reality of female experience, and the pathetic lives of women driven to the point of hysteria, escapist, sacrificial goats and highlights the compulsions which compel them to silence, suicide or death while delivering a child. Most of the time women are misunderstood because of the power accumulated by men, and they become instrumental in forcing women to silence. Women become the cause of subjugation and suffering. Urmila raises her voice against all these unregulated rules and regulations established by the male dominated society.

In the novel *A Matter of Time* a journey in women's inner life is explained. An attempt is made to understand male psychology. Gopal, who deserts his wife and children, is not condemned without consideration. Sumi reasons out that the metaphysical question of the ultimate truth of human life and the persistent human search for meaning in existence is Gopal's reasons. The novel weaves an intricate pattern of relationships within an extended family on both sides across generations. Manorama, Kalyani, Sumi and Aru belong to four generations of the same family, each representing a specific mode of experience. Manorama is a typical product of the patriarchal value system, for she resented the birth of Kalyani, her daughter, as she wanted a son. She forces a marriage between two unwilling partners, her daughter Kalyani and her younger brother Shripati and she even holds Kalyani responsible for all her sorrows and calls her an enemy. But it is Kalyani who represents the survival power of women, which tides her across her mother's ill treatment and her husband's rejection. The novelist observes "... The real miracle is Kalyani herself, who has survived intact, in spite of what Shripati did to her. Kalyani who has survived Manorama's myriad acts of cruelty". (151) There is a clear change from Manorama to Kalyani, and she says to Aru:

> My mother did not care for my children either. Daughters again, she said.... I am luckier than my mother. She is the one unlucky who didn't know how to enjoy her children and grand children. (226)

When Gopal walks out on Sumi, it appears to Kalyani like a renewal of her own life, but unlike her mother, she gives emotional support to her daughter. The struggle to learn to live alone and assert oneself against the tide of tragedy is in Sumi. She is trying to work out a strategy to withstand the shock and the emptiness left behind by Gopal, and to create a life for herself and her daughters. Aru is full of the sense of injustice and protest against her father.

If Sumi is trying to retain self-identity, Aru fights for the rights of women. The metaphysical question of the meaning of life runs as an undercurrent in the narrative. It is the emptiness of life that induces Gopal to leave his family. The narrator philosophizes that there is a great deal to be said for a belief in many lives. To think that we have only one life given to us, to know that this is all there is, and to understand the implications of this, is to be stricken by paralysis. The narrator reminds us the truth of Krishna's message to Arjun that 'we are mere instruments'. Death is seen as the final reality and the death of Sumi and Shripati endorses the belief. The novelist sums up:

> If it is indeed true that we are bound to our destinies, that there is no point struggling against them, even this remains -that we do not submit passively or cravenly, but with dignity and strength. (246)

These words have a great importance in the context of feminine discourse, which the novelist tries to place in the wider context. Her plan is to restore women's knowledge to its proper place in history. She projects and focuses on the stratagem of readjustments her female protagonists undertake in order to forge an identity of their own. They struggle to learn to become "ones own refuge" and value the fellowship of other women.

Small Remedies, is an exposition of woman's eternal struggle for her identity. Professional efforts are disclosed by the novelist in her novel. In this novel woman's desire, her relationship with her husband and the changed freedom of motherhood are expressed. Deshpande develops equilibrium between customary demands and contemporary force by renegotiating the power relations in an attempt to resolve the crisis. Savitri Bai Indorekar's bold and rebellious act to run away from her family, her love for music is not an isolated, whimsical and individual decision. Bande Usha in her essay, *'A Matter of Time'* and *'Small Remedies'* expresses her views regarding the love for music:

> The love for music transcends personal borders and becomes a part of the key social and political agendas undertaken by the late nineteenth century women such as Pandit Ramabai, Anandi Bai Joshi, Kashi Bai Kanitkar, Tara Bai Sinde, to name a few, who had the courage to stand up against the oppressive social regime. (193)

Madhu, the protagonist-biographer is a very strong character. She exercises her choices, rejects her husband's ideology of essentialist approach and rebuilds her emotional, creative, imaginative and realistic 'self'. By writing the biography of Savitri Bai Indorekar's as a challenge, she exercises her artistic and intellectual capacities. Writing itself is an act of empowerment. She knows that where there is power there is resistance. The female characters in the novel try to live life on their own terms, resisting its changes with stony silence. Art is beyond caste, class or religion. Bai comes from an orthodox Brahmin family; Gulam Saab and Hasina are Muslims, Hasina sings Akka Mahadevi's vachanas at the musical concerts. Hence, at the altar of music they have but one faith -music. Politics creates problems, not art. Deshpande resists the poisonous fangs of politics.

Shashi Deshapande's novel *Moving On,* published in 2004, studies how women with all difficulties in life have to move on. This novel has a complex narrative structure that has, using memory, experience and written texts, the diaries of the dead. Shashi Deshpande says, "Memories and pictures of the past, dreams, hopes and plans for the future -these are as real to us as the present". (Deshpande: *Literary Review)* The novel is a family story of intimate distances, of emotional wounds and of intrusions. The domestic atmosphere quite harmonious and sanctified by the standard norms of the society is often seen with disagreement, supremacy and infringement. The complex nature of human relationships is analyzed, whether it is within a family or in the broader social space. The novelist knits her narration around multiple acts of transgression bringing in the conflict of selves, other man, other women, physical, emotional, sexual, ethical, individual and social binaries. The novel, among other things is all about 'writing'. Writing here in the novel doesn't mean autobiographical reflections; the novelist very strongly resists any such thing. Manjari in Moving On says about her father's writing: "It's easy to think that he wrote in his diary as a counter to his loneliness, that he was, in fact, communicating with himself". (21)

Writing gives a particular shape and voice to one's ideas and feelings. Manjari's mother, Vasu, is a real writer of romanticized marriage stories published in popular Marathi magazines. She wrote such stuff that she, herself, did not believe in writing, had become a substitute for her lived experience, a world full of make-belief atmosphere

In all societies, a woman is culturally assigned certain norms of behavior such as standards of conduct, taste and decorum; any deviation from or violation of the ideal image of womanhood, makes her an unruly, obstinate woman to be condemned by society. But a woman is forced by man to accept the status of an inferior compared to that of man; hence, women must struggle against male controlled institutions and ideologies; must have solidarity among themselves, by biological instincts. Hence, in order both to gain equality and to realize their human potential, women must become autonomous.

The novel, as a fictional narrative, should be placed in the 'in-between space of relations autonomy'. Manjari refuses to marry Raj, fights back the property mafia and learns to drive her own car -a clear indication of her resistance to patriarchal domination. As a woman, Manjari could not betray her desire and the physical demands of her body. Her sexual relations with her tenant, in her full command of the situation, as she wants "eternal conflict between man and woman, the man asserting his right, claiming his right to her body, the female denying him". (276) And she claims her own body. Manjari shows how Deshpande wants women to be themselves, and not owned and claimed by men. Raj represents the voice of patriarchy trying to identify the female, as done earlier, whereas Manjari challenges the essential idea of female identity as male, and leaves the door open for social and cultural change. Her engagements with life allow her to take up the middle path -be yourself and allow others to be; live on your own terms and let others live on their own.

In the Country of Deceit (2008) is the latest novel in which Shashi Deshpande depicts the feelings of love. The novel is a love story which travels around the oily, treacherous surroundings that love holds people in. Devayani chooses to live alone in her new house in the small town Rajnur after her parents' death, ignoring the gently voiced disapproval of her family and friends. Teaching English, creating a garden and making friends, Devayani meets Ashok Chinappa, Rajnur's New District Superintendent of Police. Devayani, as a "New Woman" faces the hurdles of life bravely.

Devayani's falling in love with Ashok, a police officer who is older and married, with a 10-year-old daughter, and they suddenly embark on a passionate affair is an open challenge not only to the members of her family: Savi, her sister, Sindhu and other members but also to the whole society. Savi opposes but Devi ignores her quenching of physical thirst through sexual love. But after some time she starts feeling alienated herself. As she herself says:

> First I had been a follower of my spirited, beautiful older sister, then in charge of parents' lives, the observer of their tragedy. For a brief while I had acted as my cousin Kshama's helper and later I had been Sindhu's attendant after surgery now, for the first time, I had to play solo. I had no one else to look after, no one to think about. (8).

Devayani considers the love with Ashok more than sex. She realizes that her love with Ashok is temporary; therefore, she thinks that she has to take a strong decision to be apart from him. However, she knows that it is wrong to go with Ashok in love; she keeps him in her memory and does not want to forget him. She challenges her family saying that there are no boundaries for love. Ashok becomes the Boon hero, tough but tender, whom Devayani typically resists but soon he becomes her "sun, moon and stars". He visits her furtively and showers her with love and passionate embraces, but Devayani cannot accept the role of a "whore" or a "floozy" and now she realizes that she must stop this. They can't go on. They must stop. She will stop, she won't go on with this, she must tell Ashok she can't go on, she will tell him it's over.

Freedom for the Indian woman means freedom from centuries of male-domination and male-ordained social and cultural norms. In fact, since antiquity man has viewed woman as someone inferior to him. Women were not allowed any identity and individuality of their own. They were reduced to the status of a slave and forced to serve the patriarchal society. Even today, to some extent, they are valued only if they conform to the male demands. But today's woman is striving much for her identity or authorization. They have realized that their inferiority is not ordained in heaven and gender is neither natural nor unchallengeable because it is the creation of patriarchy.

Now they have become intolerant of their exploitation and victimization by men and have revolted against sexual politics and gender arrangements. Woman is in herself a power. Be a woman supplementary aptitude from the God or the additional ability of procreation provided by the God to woman. She is a perfect creature of God. No other creature is as whole as woman. Man is a nonentity in himself. What is man? Where does he come from? The answer is as simple as that it is the woman who creates the man. That is why the woman is considered to be more persuasive than man. In Rig Veda there are three deities i.e. "BRAHMA', 'VISHNU' AND 'MAHESH', symbolizing 'CREATOR', 'PRESERVER' and 'DESTROYER". 'BRAHMA' is equivalent to 'MOTHER' who as creator of 'SRISTI' is a woman. Therefore she should be considered just like God. 'FATHER' is considered to be a 'PRESERVER' and 'DEATH' is considered to be 'DESTROYER'. Again there is an old saying that the labourer mother who is a woman is better than a millionaire father because the father being a millionaire is not capable to look after his offspring appropriately and a mother, in spite of being a labourer, can oversee her children better. Hence, saying that woman is frail is doing injustice not only with woman but with God also. Today's woman is not a woman of Shakespeare who describes woman in *Hamlet* in the words: "Frailty, thy name is woman!" (1.ii.146), not the woman of Hindi poet Kabirdas who says:

> Nari Ke Zhai Parat Andha Hot Bhujang
> Kabira Unki Kya Gati Jo Nit Nari Ke Sang.

If he means to say that we should not remain in the company of woman, it is a trivial facile, because the place of a child is in the lap of his mother who is a 'Nari'. A married man always remains in the company of his wife called 'Ardhangini,' that is, she again is a 'Nari'. Today's woman is not a woman of the Rig Veda which avers: "Lord Indra himself has said that woman has very little intelligence. She cannot be taught (8/33/17)." In Yajur Veda (Taitriya Samhita) we read: "Women code says that the women are without energy (6/5/8/2)." In the present scenario all these things have become superseded.

It is a fact that the woman of today no longer wants to be a Cinderella, a Lachingada, and a Madison. But she wants to be Kalpana Chawla, Bachendari Pal and Kiran Bedi etc. who have touched the crest of success. Today, the suppressed female voice is articulated. To a certain extent, the dignity of woman is affirmed. She has a greater share of social responsibility and a greater readiness to author her own authority.

The woman of today is educated and exposed to Western ideas. She is intensely aware of the injustice heaped on her. She does not believe that woman is an inferior being in any way and must remain passive and submissive. She is waking up to the releasing knowledge that there is more to life than dependency on husband or parents and social acceptance. The woman is self-sufficient in all aspects. The only need for woman is to feel self-assured, assert herself, be self-reliant and have holistic-solidarity. The biggest inadequacy for women empowerment is no other than the lack of solidarity among them. They do not bond with one another.

Thus, the new woman is inching towards freedom and she has been trying to learn bonding with one another. She concentrates on the theme of meaninglessness and sexual confusion suffered by her in tradition-oriented society, asserting thereby that the inequality of sexes is neither a biological given, nor a divine mandate, but a cultural construct. She is aware that her life is a succession of traps created by mothers, lovers and finally herself, by accepting the confinement of marriage. She is for self-fulfillment and full development of woman's varied faculties -physical, emotional, moral, and intellectual.

Works Cited

Beauvior de Simonne. *The Second Sex*. Ed. and Tans. H.M. Parshley. Harmondsworth: Penguin Book, 1972.

Deshpande, Shashi. *Come Up and Be Dead*. New Delhi: Vikas Vikas Publishing House, 2003.

_________. *The Dark Holds No Terrors*. Delhi: Penguin Books, 2003.

_________. *That Long Silence*. Delhi: Penguin Books, 1988.

_________. *A Matter of Time*. New Delhi: Penguin, 1996.

_________. *Moving On*. New Delhi: Penguin/ Viking, 2004.

_________. *In The Country of Deceit*. New Delhi: Viking/ Penguin, 2008.

Band, Usha. "A Matter of Time and Small Remedies: *Writing 'Difference*." *The Novels of Shashi Deshpande*. Ed. Chanchala.K. Naik. Delhi: Pencraft International, 2005.

Literary Review, The Hindu 15th Sept, 2004.

7

Shashi Deshpande: A Unique Indian Novelist

Arvind Kumar Sharma and *Suman Lata*

Shashi Deshpande is purely an Indian by soul as she has presented authentic mentality of India through her novels. Born in Dharwad in Karnataka in 1938 and the winner of Sahitya Academy Award in 1990, Shashi Deshpande is one of the most popular fictionists in Indian English Literature. Her soul wears a mantle of complete and unique Indianness. She has emphasized on futility of segregating past and present tradition in her novels. Her themes and characters vary from novel to novel. Though she repudiates any kind of labeling of her fiction in terms of gender, politics or ideology yet social criticism and Indianness have remained the pivot of her fiction. Commenting on the otherness of her fiction, M. K. Naik observes:

> Her writing is clearly part of Indian literature, and emerges from her rootedness in middle class Indian society. Understatement is the hallmark of her work; she never indulges in verbal pyrotechnics, her lucid prose never attracts attention to itself by using Indian words. Nor is she interested in the

> exotic aspects of India; there are no Maharajahs, tiger hunts and holy men in her work. (163)

Shashi Deshpande herself says in an interview with Lakshmi Holmstorm:

> ....I am different from other Indians who write in English, my background is very firmly there. I was never educated abroad. My novels don't have any Westerners, for example. They are just about Indian people and the complexities of our lives, our inner lives and our outer lives and reconciliation between them. My English is as we use it, I don't make it easier for anyone really. If I make any change, it's because I think the novel needs it not because the readers need it. (163-164)

Suffice it to say Shashi Deshpande's background has been purely Indian. Though her father, Sriranga, was a Kannad dramatist as well as a great Sanskrit scholar, Shashi Deshpande has chosen to write in English with unique Indian soul. Her all works, full of realism, more practical and authentic in Indian context, reveal the fact that she herself has experienced all types of Indian situations. In the reply of 'Is she conscious of any literary tradition that influenced her writing?' asked by Bijay Kumar Das in a conversation, Shashi Deshpande says:

> I guess all writers are influenced by the literary traditions of the language they write in. However, for me, like for so many Indian writers who write in English, there was this gap between the traditions of the language I wrote in and the literary traditions of the society I was living in. (322)

She has been very careful to authenticate the Indian characters and situations in her all novels. Even she has elucidated and perused the other writers too in this regard. In a conversation with Bijay Kumar Das, She says:

> ....I don't understand the view that English writers

> have failed to authenticate Indian characters and situations in their writings. There are good and bad writers in all languages. And I thought we had left the bogey of 'authenticity' far behind. Do my novels have to prove their Indianness even today? (325)

She is filled with the lore of Indianness, as the themes presented in her novels are living and much more practical in Indian context. Being an Indian lady, she has experienced every type of feelings and emotions of Indian women especially of middle class. She herself states: "I don't like to call myself a feminist writer. I say I 'm a feminist, but I don't write to propagate an ism."

In her thematic preoccupations and fictional techniques she has definitely marked an advance over many well-known Indian women writers viz Anita Desai, Kamala Markandey and Nayantara Sahgal. She clarifies her position in the context of the global feminist movements and expresses the view that no amount of theorizing can solve the real and genuine human problems that a woman faces in a male dominated society. In an interview to Lakshmi Holmstorm, Deshpande says:

> Feminism is not a matter of theory. It is difficult to apply Kate Millett or Simone de Beauvoir or whoever to the reality of our daily lives in India, and then there are such terrible misconceptions about feminism by people here.... And I actually feel that a lot of women in India are feminists without realizing it. (132-133)

Social responsibilities or social commitments have been the main and unavoidable themes of all Indian writers and Deshpande is not an exception. Her all novels are about women and exposition to understand them, their history, their place, their role in the family as well as in the society and, above all, their relationship with others. Especially Deshpande has elucidated various images of women in Indian context. Through her novels she has awakened the long silence of women.

As a true representative of Indian life and culture, Deshpande's novels describe the authentic situations of present India. Besides dealing with the mythological characters, she also interprets the culture and philosophy of today through the modern characters. Through the medium of foreign tongue, she very successfully interprets the spirit of India to the west. She presents, with deep love and affection, with force and vigour, and with a detective sense, the modern and complicated situations especially concerned with middle class educated family through her novels. She has perused every aspect of Indian woman. She declares it undoubtedly. A man co-operates and uplifts the woman in society in all respects but he does not like the woman's progress at the cost of superseding his dominancy. Like the sub-theme of 'Three Idiots' when a woman fails, the man feels sorry but if she supersedes him, he does not tolerate it.

Sublimity is the soul of Indian culture. Deshpande has followed this through sublime characters of her novels. A diehard feminist cannot see beyond the narrow prism of her woman centred vision and it is for nothing that She occupies a unique position in the galaxy of the contemporary Indian English novelists. Meenakshi Mukharjee rightly says:

> While accepting the Shahitya Academy Award about a decade ago Shashi Deshpande had expressed her importance with reviewers who routinely used words like 'sensitivity' and 'sensibility' if the writer happened to be a woman. She said she herself thought of her work in terms of strength. ... Shashi Deshpande's early novels were published just at the time the post Midnight's Children generation of writers was becoming big news. Since she refused to play by global rules, she could not be included in this league. The only

> other exportable slot the media could think of was the champion of the oppressed women. But anyone who has read her novels carefully knows that her special value lies elsewhere- in an uncompromising toughness, in her attempts to do what has never been attempted in English, her insistence on being read on her own terms and a refusal to be packaged according to the demands of the market. (The Hindu, May 07, 2000)

India is in her heart, her thoughts, her feelings, her stories, her novels, imagery and personality. Every aspect, manner, trend, style used in her works is never untouched with Indianness. Even the music she uses in her novels is Indian (Hindustani), though it does not blend with English writing. In this context in an interview to T. Vijay Kumar, Shashi Deshpande says:

> I really had no choice because I am more familiar with Hindustani music. When I think of music, I only think of Hindustani music. So I could not have used carnatic music. But if I had used carnatic music where the Shahitya is very much a part of the music, I would not have been able to say, as I do somewhere in the novel, that when Savitribai sings, the words are not important at all, because she compresses her emotions through the singing itself, through the raga, not the words. (http//ch.8m.com)

Works Cited

Naik, MK & Narayan, Shyamala A. "A Room of Their Own: Women Novelists." *Indian English Literature 1980-2000, A Critical Study*. Delhi: Pencraft International, 2001.

Deshpande, Shashi. "A Conversation with Bijay kumar Das". *The Indian Journal of English Studies*, Vol. XLVI, 2009.

________. "An Interview to Lakshmi Holmstorm", *Wasafiri*, 17, 1993). *The Indian Journal of English Studies*, Vol. XLVI, 2009.

________. "An Interview to Lakshmi Holmstorm", *Wasafiri*, 17, 1993). *The Indian Journal of English Studies*, Vol. XLIV, 2007.

________. "An Interview to T Vijay Kumar". http// ch.8m.com.

Mukharjee, Meenakshi. "On Her Own Terms- A Review of *Small Remedies*", *The Hindu*, May 07, 2000.

8

Nayantara Sahgal's Pro-feminist approach

Laxman Yadav

A blue blooded personality with a strong political family back up, a well- known social elitist, and at the same time a noted national movement activist, journalist-turned-writer, Mrs. Nayantara Sahgal is still today a well-known 'feminist' in the world of Indian English literature. By now she has written and lectured on burning and relevant topics for the intellectuals in India and abroad. She is known as a writer with strong political consciousness throughout the academic world.

Her multi-faceted personality is reflected in her various writings: fictonal and non-fictional in English, eg. *A Time to be Happy (1958), This Time of Morning (1968), Storm in Chandigarh (1969), The Day in Shadow (1971), A Situation in New Delhi (1977), A Voice of Freedom (1977), Indira Gandhi's Emergence and Style (1978), Indira Gandhi, Her Road to Power (1982), Rich Like Us (1985), Plans for Departure (1985), Mistaken Identity (1988), Lesser Breeds* (2003) and *Before Freedom;* which are written right from 1950s to 2000s.

Nayantara Sahgal's pro-feminist stance is reflected in

female characters' psyche viz. *A Situation in New Delhi, Rich Like Us, Plans for Departure* etc. A study of the novels is likely to bring about her skill in revealing the women's inner feelings, struggle and escape.

Sahgal has a close look at the romantic falsification of man-woman relationship, pre-marital as well as extra-marital relationships, going through the nadir of perplexed mental situation of the victim especially woman from the educational background trapped in the east-west cultural confrontation in India, both in stereotyped and so- called liberal families. She has emphasized the sole interest of ones, in exploiting socially vulnerable women. She has also presented the opposite sex's yearnings very beautifully as one may feel while reading a scene mentioned in her *Storm in Chandigarh* and others too.

Thus through her novels she wants to give a message to the society that in the country like India women's vulnerability is not just because of the prejudices by the males but also because of static women themselves. So, oppressed women have been suffering double punishments by the both sexes under which they have to sustain their lives.

In *Rich Like Us,* especially in the portrayal of Sonali Ranade, we notice the feminist in Sahgal. *Rich Like Us,* coming after an interval of seven years marks the third and the most mature phase of Sahgal's career. The women belonging to this phase are strong-willed and emotionally independent. They refuse to bow before the stranglehold of men, right from the beginning. They are mistresses of indomitable spirit. Sonali grows up with a dream to fulfil, "a new tradition to create, her independent worth to prove." (28) An uncompromising administrative officer, she refuses to pretend that "the emperor's new clothes were beautiful." (28) Her survival instinct is strong and instead of giving in, she gives up. Her resignation is not her acceptance of defeat; it is rather her defiance against oppressive forces, her refusal to cringe before forces acting against her identity. It is her unique manner of asserting her individuality.

The thirst for identity is not a problem faced by the Indian Women only. Anna Hansen of *Plans for Departure* is a Danish woman, free from the shackles that women in a parochial society face, yet she comes to India when she wants to "break out" and be herself. She is despaired to think of her epitaph as:

> Here lies Anna, beloved wife, who died without having made much effort to live, and nobody noticed the difference, since being a beloved wife was supposed to be reward enough. (62)

Her zeal for emancipation forces her to leave the warm embraces not only of home but also of a country. She'd rather face hostilities in a foreign land than be a slave in her own surroundings, to her own people. Here is a woman whose visions of self-assertion are not clouded by conventions. She knows not only what she wants but also how to achieve it.

In her article, "Women's Liberation: The Indian Way," Sahgal recognises 'women-power' but laments that Indian society has still not accepted this notion. Ours is a patriarchal society where personality is a luxury for women. The need of the time is:

> A whole new look at woman "not as the property of father, husband or son, and dependent on their bounty but as valuable human material to be brought to full flower and full participation in her life and events. (6)

Sahgal's concept of emancipation reaches its culmination duly and justly in her last novel, *Mistaken Identity*. Here we meet a woman who is out and out a rebel. The Rani of Vijaygarh defies all moulds and definitions. She is a class apart. She breaks all boundaries and makes her own rules. Sahgal's other young and so-called emancipated women need to learn a lesson or two from their successor the Rani, though she belongs to an age when women were expected to stay behind veil. The woman is herself confined in multiple chains. First, there is the hierarchy, then there is her wifehood to a Raja, and then again there is the veil behind which she is doomed to choke. This woman shines in the firmament of Sahgal's fiction as the pole star, the brightest and the most firm. Here is a woman, who is living in 1920-30s, is uneducated, rather illiterate, has an apathetic husband, has nothing to look forward to, and yet she dares to shun her husband from her life, when she discovers that the man has no respect for her kind. There are no outside forces which make her aware of this (like Vishal for Saroj), there is no one to support her in her crusade against female exploitation (like Raj for Simrit), and yet she dares to challenge the authority of her husband in his own home. Exhibiting exemplary strength of character the woman behind the veil breaks all ties with her husband, when he marries for the third time. Though she knows nothing about women's liberation, she becomes a strong practitioner of the same because whatever measures she takes to insulate her self-respect from tyrannical forces; she does so without the support of anyone else. It is her inherent courage, her strength, her own will-power. This she does not owe to any Vishal, Raj or Usman.

This unrelenting soul prostrates before the deities to procure a child not because she considers it essential for hierarchy but because she wants to express herself through it. Her pining for a child is symbolic of her search for identity. It's not as a wife or as a mother that she is satisfied; she has to survive as a person. Even her fascination with superhuman powers is an expression of her preoccupation with emancipation. Power in all forms is welcome because power rules the roost. When in the end she breaks free from all inhibitions and marries comrade Yusuf, it is without any infesting sense of guilt that she does so. Her marriage to comrade Yusuf, then, is not an effort to seek refuge from the evils that the Raja has subjected her to. Such refuge, she does not ask for. This woman does not need support even from her son,

Bhushan. She walks her own proud way even when there is no comrade Yusuf in her life. Sahgal shows a steady evolution in the course of her writing career. Rani of Vijaygarh, though a nameless character, marks the culmination of the onward march of Sahgal's new woman towards freedom. Anna Hansen, of *Plans for Departure* is a free woman no doubt, but given the environs and conditions, Rani of Vijaygarh is nonpareil in her spirit of defiance and propensity to assert. This woman may well compete with other feminist characters on the scene.

Sahgal, though not a militant feminist, feels strongly about female-exploitation and male sarcasm toward the issue of women's identity crises. She demands social justice for women, her focus being on freedom. Sahgal's fictional women challenge the moth-eaten pretence of tradition without suffering from loss of identity: "On the contrary they seem to gain or acquire some kind of individuality". (Talwar 103) They threaten the stranglehold of men and reaffirm their faith in their potentials. The battle that starts quite demurely with Maya keeps advancing and gathering momentum through Rashmi, Saroj, Simrit and Devi and in Sonali it reaches its culmination. Anna and the Rani take it to its glorious heights. Rashmi Talwar's suggestion seems to overlook the powerful presence of the Rani:

> It may be desirable for women writers in the future to portray a woman who does not adhere to or follow any model but is herself initiated into a search to discover her deeper identity. (104)

This is precisely what Sahgal's hitherto last creation the Rani does. In her person the concept of women's quest for identity reaches its zenith and we have good reasons to believe that should Sahgal give us another novel, the female protagonist therein would certainly be unparalleled in her self-determination and self-assertion. Talwar's observation: "....from the vantage point of the twenty-first century, Sahgal's pioneering quest for woman's emancipation will, no doubt be a momentous literary document of the present era," (104) seems the most apt peroration of the issue.

Although its publication coincided with the rise of women's lib in the West, Sahgal's *The Day in a Shadow* is not a feminist novel. In fairness to her, it was not even intended to be one. It is a woman's novel. It gives a sensitive account of the suffering of women in India and indeed has a whole lot of data which could have gone into the making of a feminist novel. It gives a sensitive account of the suffering of women in Indian society. Sahgal reveals the suffering caused by men but does not advocate a separatist stance. Even though many of her women opt out of marriage, yet they look for happiness and self-fulfilment again in a world shared by both the sexes. The call is for recognition of the woman as an equally important partner in marriage or in any other relationships. Her needs, her freedom, her personality, her individuality should be equally valued. In her novel, *This Time of Morning*, Mira is shocked to know about the failure of the marriage of Rashmi. According to her, suffering was a part of life and in every condition women should stay married. Ironically, it is Rashmi's father who understands his daughter and supports her to lead a life of her own. Sahgal delineates with keen perception and sensitivity the problems and sufferings of women in marriage. The women feel entrapped, oppressed and doomed to the chores of husband and home. Some accept their fate and others get desperate for freedom. They reject the stereotype and prefer separation just to live a more meaningful life, a life of self-fulfilment. However, ultimately we find in her novels a strong plea for the preservation of the tradition of a family. In this she invites men to make their contribution. The existing set-up with its uneven power division will continue to bring suffering to women. And as long as one half of humanity suffers, we cannot hope for a better world. Nayantara Sahgal envisions a world which should be based on equality, sharing and harmony between the two sexes where the need, the functions, the virtues of women are valued equally along with those of men. Their vision, thus, is identical with that of feminists like Marilyn French, Dale Spender, Lynne Seagal who also ask for a world built on equality of sexes, where male and female, masculine and feminine are valued equally.

Nayantara Sahgal places her women characters, mostly with good educational background, in conflict with a parochial society and depicts their struggle to pop out of their shells. Though there is much about suffering within marriage, yet we also get a glimpse of the attempts made to condition her personality along sexist lines before marriage. Betty Friedan, in her book, *the Feminine Mystique,* suggested that a woman can find fulfillment in only some creative work of her own. Sahgal shares the idea, where she suggests that a person should pursue his art whether it is writing a book or sewing a table cloth. In *This Time of Morning,* Nita too has a thirst to do something of her own. Her parents are a queer blend of Eastern and western culture. Her father drinks, dances and attends clubs, but when it comes to the daughter, she is not allowed to move unescorted. Nita is married to Vijay, against her wishes. She is not happy and finds pleasure with Kalyan. Sahgal strongly attacks such convention and names it as "just organized rape." In another place, she condemns such attitudes which value women as property and discourage individuality in them.

With Leela, another character of *This Time of Morning,* the situation is different. She manages to go to America but, here this "modest, unpretentious" member of the Hindu family commits suicide when she realizes that she is pregnant. The novelist shows her concern with the question how far different conventions and traditions imply a fundamental difference in moral outlook. How can one accept Western culture without losing her integrity and independence? Where pre-marital relationship is considered an unpardonable crime for girls, there is no explanation for the extra-marital relationship of a man in an Indian society. This is what Sahgal has tried to portray in *Storm in Chandigarh*. Inder brutally tortures Sarjo for her premarital relationship with one of her friends at college. In *A Situation in New Delhi*, when Madhu is raped by a group of university students, she has no solace even from her parents. In hospital when she cries for mercy and justice, she is cupped over by the nurse. The nurse puts her hand on Madhu's mouth to keep quiet, may be a symbolic gesture to convey that the victimized women have to suffer in silence and that the cries would only lead to a scandal and make matters worse.

Girls like Pinky, Tazi and Reba cherish a rosy picture of marriage and are unaware of the obligation involved in this relationship, the relationship which is full of complex problems of understanding adjustments, etc. in marriage. They are care-free as birds. Society considers such girls as excellent and they comfortably fit in. However, such characters as Pinky remain minor characters. The central character in Sahgal's novels is a thinking woman striving for an individual, independent personality. Sahgal confronts a number of issues, with particular interest in the condition of women who are positioned at different levels in the class structure. Her female characters are not strong. Their lives run in such a way that they resist the limitations of the definition of "women" which circumscribes their identity. By using English as her medium of expression, Sahgal indubitably belongs to an elite circle and yet she is able to give voice to the marginalized figure of Indian society, mainly women. She poses a strong counter-voice to the dominant patriarchal narrative which has subdued women's role to the absolute minimum. Her novels not only offer the struggle and coverage of women but also a condemnatory view of the practices of the patriarchal society.

Conclusively, speaking about Sahgal's pro-feminist approach, she has exhibited her inner sub-consciousness feeling vulnerable situation of the Women victims whether one is rich or poor, educational or not. She also expresses the sighs of pre-marital lechery shown by their male counterparts as well as extra-marital non-compatibility with the spouses especially fell by the female counterparts. Somewhere she smartly expresses the half-hiddenly expressed affairs between the two bonvivants from the male-female sexes as one counterpart has equal fires for the other. Nayantara Sahgal has observed all such vicious acts of the society with her micro-eyes which are today always discussed by the social pundits. Thus we can say that what she said yesterday we are following these days.

Works Cited

Sahgal, Nayantara. *Rich Like Us*. London: Sceptre, 1987.

________. *Plans for Departure*. London: Penguin, 1987.

________. *Point of View*. New Delhi: Prestige, 1997.

________. "Women's Libration: The Indian Way," *The Sundary Standard*, 1971 (21 March).

________. *A Situation in New Delhi*. London: Magazine Editions, 1977.

________. "'Women: Persons or Possession," *Hindustan Times (Sunday Magazine)*, 19th July 1970.

Talwar, Sree Rashmi. *Woman's Space: The Mosaic World of Margaret Drabble and Nayantara Sahgal*. New Delhi: Creative Books, 1997.

9

Woman's Battle for Identity in Manju Kapur's *Difficult Daughters*

Indu Swami

Indian English fiction constitutes an important part of the world literature today, and women novelists have made significant contributions to it. The post-colonial women writers interpreted and rewrote issues related to pre and post-colonial experiences as they appeared on the stage of Indian English Literature. They started portraying emotional and psychological themes on par with the partition experience in general and by referring them to women's experience thereby adding a gender perspective to the issues related to partition. Works focusing on aspects related to partition exposed the critical, differential dimension and the impact of partition on men and women with substantial light being focused on the reality of the relation between gender and socio-historical processes, as Seema Malik writes:

> History of women may not necessarily be the same as the history of men. The impact of cataclysmic event like partition on women was much different and more traumatic and enduring than men. The word partition is inadequate to encompass the

> myriad meanings this event has for women or to even approximate the many levels of experiences that they lived. (Malik 184)

The life, women lived and struggled under the oppressive mechanism of a closed society was reflected in the writings of women writers in the post-colonial India. Manju Kapur has also knitted her first novel, *Difficult Daughters* with the same fabric as the backdrop and emerged as a significant novelist on the contemporary literary scene. The present paper aims at exploring the theme of women's struggle for their existence in the novel. Perfectly set around the times of independence and partition, this novel clearly explains that the concept of modernity involves partition. It relates the story of a young woman, Virmati, torn between filial responsibilities, desire for education and emancipation and her delinquent love towards a married professor of English named Harish. It portrays a woman's need to be loved, to be needed, meaningfully by the mother, as a young daughter, in her parental family, in her youth, by a man and lastly in her married life.

From *Tretayuga* till date, woman has never been in a position to demand or at least expect the ideal state from her male counterpart who deliberately forgets his own responsibilities but expects the qualities of an ideal wife such as *Kaaryashyu dasi,... Karaneshu mantri* etc. From the ancient times to the recent ones, women have been constantly under the pressure of living up to these expectations. This tendency inevitably leads to conflict which woman has to face with until she finds a way out. This conflict and the resultant rift in man-woman relationship are clearly and completely shown in the *Difficult Daughters*.

The novel clearly shows the dilemma of women who carry the burden of being female as well as the added responsibility of being mothers to a number of their own sex. Theirs is a world torn between tradition and modernity, colonial upbringings and the disquieting presence of the freedom movements, and these women amidst the backdrop of chaos and confusion try to search for security not only for themselves but also for their daughters, who threaten to break out of the mould from time to time.

As the eldest daughter of a joint business family located at Amritsar in Punjab of the pre-partition India, Virmati is burdened with the task of looking after her horde of brothers and sisters apart from her regular course of study. Being the eldest of the eleven children, she has to play the role of a second mother for her brothers and sisters. She yearns for affection, for some sign that she is special. But never gets any. She has hectic schedule of caring of the siblings, to run the house and helping her sick mother. Yet she never receives love nor is showered affection, though her heart yearns much for it. Her mother without any apparent reason often abuses her. Her relationship with her mother is most problematic. This is because Kasturi, the mother sees in her a rival able to challenge her world. Besides Kasturi's repeated pregnancies make her sickly resulting in her total dependence on Virmati to manage her household. As a natural consequence, her unique position in the home is lost which she has to yield to her daughter quite unwillingly. Virmati thus becomes a "substitute" and not the "double" that every mother wants her daughter to be. As a consequence the relationship assumes hostile dimensions:

> ...why was her daughter so restless all the time? In a girl, that spelt disaster. Virmati left raging. Why was anything to her mother so difficult? May be it was best to keep silent. (11)

Though she runs the entire household single-handedly, she does not get due recognition, not to mention of love and affection. She wants to pursue her education further, but her parents intend to marry her soon. "It seemed to Virmati that her family could talk of nothing else but her wedding. Every word they said had so little relation to her inner life..." (19).

She finds demarcation line at every free step of hers; it is this forbidding situation at home that draws her near to the professor. The professor encourages her to go further with her studies and her academic association with the professor results into their amorous relationship. And as it comes to the notice of her family, she is accused of loose morals and is punished by shutting her in the large dark room. She becomes a stigma to the face of her family; all the senior members of family boycott her. She finds her sacrifices for the family futile and unavailing; her one wrong step has drifted her from the core of her family.

Here is the predicament of a young educated woman who is enlightened enough to want to reach beyond the boundaries of her home and long for her own space, yet not liberated enough to know how to go about it without hurting others. In Virmati, one finds a desperate yearning for a way of life which would give her freedom and some sort of identity. Even when she finds courage to voice her desire to her mother, she is considered irresponsible, ungrateful and self-centred, and is told in no uncertain terms "you are forgetting what comes first...at your age I was already expecting you not fighting with my mother" (19). Unfortunately, she has neither a mother figure nor the presence of a confidante with whom she can share her trauma and pain. Kasturi rejects any outward expression of love, as "the language of feeling" (11) has never flown between them.

Feminists emphatically insists on the importance of women becoming "aware" of themselves as individuals and shaping their own destinies by assertiveness and self-confidence and use the term "feminist consciousness" or "consciousness raising" in this context. Juliet Mitchell defines consciousness raising as "the process of transforming the hidden, individual fears of women into a shared awareness of the meaning of them as social problems, the release of anger, anxiety, the struggle of proclaiming the painful and transforming it into the political" (Mitchell, 61). While the traditional-minded women accept their false conditioning into sub-ordination and dependence without demur, the sensitive and aware women realize need for individuality and revolt against the established norms and traditions. In her individual need for love, Virmati too rebels against tradition. She is impelled by the inner need to feel love as an individual rather than as a responsible daughter. She has plunged into a dedicated effort to carve an identity for herself.

Standing on the threshold of the country's freedom, Manju Kapur's protagonist takes her first faltering step towards her own independence, without being aware of the pitfalls or the fact that freedom always comes with a price. The mother, instead of encouraging and supporting her daughter, spurns her every attempt to assert herself. In her daughter's life she represents the tradition bound reality with her sometimes silent, sometimes demanding presence, and acts as the guardian of her virtues. As a result, the daughter goes through various degrees of neglect, humiliation, withdrawal and alienation. Explaining the complex relationship between the two, Simone de Beauvoir comments:

> In the daughter, the mother does not hail a member of the superior caste; in her she seeks a double. She projects upon her daughter all the ambiguity of her relation with herself; and when, the otherness of this 'alter ego' manifests itself, the mother feels herself betrayed. (Beauvoir 533)

The mother's inability to understand her daughter's restlessness, leads her to distrust the role of education, as she considers it a corrupting influence in her daughter's life. Kasturi, when faced with Virmati's refusal to marry, questions, "What kind of learning was this that deprived her of her reason?" (55), and wonders, "How had girls changed so much in just a generation?" (55). Kasturi remembers her own childhood when she was sent to school, against her mother's wishes, as a part of Arya Samaj's reform movement, where "she learned reading, writing, balancing household accounts and sewing" (57) never forgetting in the meantime that "marriage was her destiny" (57).

In the patriarchal Indian society, marriage is a means of deliverance from being socially condemned, and it relieves a woman from the sense of insecurity and uncertainty. To the older generation, marriage is no reason to rebel; it was always accepted as a part of life's pleasure, and was a phase of initiating certain *Dharmas* associated with social and religious institutions.

The new education and close observation of the life of Kasturi generate a new urge and emotion in Virmati to get herself free from the bondage of patriarchy that denies or deserts her freedom and choice. Education in itself is viewed as a modernizing force and as an agency of change. The education versus marriage argument is reiterated many times in the novel, but with Virmati getting permission to study further, one is forced to accept that the changing times brought more and better educational opportunities for women. Virmati does not seriously view the point of education and profession as means to achieve individual freedom. But on the other hand, Shakuntala, though hails from the same background is intelligent enough to chalk out and shape up her own life, by making use of her education and very firmly resists the family's pressure for her marriage by making her priorities in life clear and she wins her independence. Virmati's life, according to her mother, is only meant to be a wife and a mother, are the consciously inculcated ideas of the Indian feminine role. As Veena Singh writes: "For Virmati herself education is an escape...an escape from the reproaches of her family and from her mother's silent disapproval" (Singh 165).

Kasturi is in no mood to recognize the need for freedom which her grown up daughter is craving for. Her intense identification with Virmati makes her think of her daughter's expression of independence as sheer selfishness smacking of ingratitude. Here Kasturi unknowingly becomes the voice of patriarchy. She holds those values as ideal which patriarchy has taught her to be so. And when her daughter rebels against such values she takes it to be a rebellion against her own self. In Kapur's novel, it is not only the daughters but also the mothers, who are difficult- difficult to please, difficult to communicate with. They are the ones who burden their daughters with unnatural demands and expectations, thus hampering their growth as individuals. As Simone de Beauvoir points out:

Most women simultaneously demand and detest their feminine condition, they live it through in a state of resentment- vexed at having produced a woman, the mother greets her with this ambiguous curse: "you shall be a woman". She hopes to compensate for her inferiority by making a superior creature out of one whom she regards as her double, and she.... Sometimes she tries to impose on the child exactly her own fate: "what was good enough for me is good enough for you, I was brought up this way, you shall share my lot. (Beauvoir 533-34)

In the Indian social set up daughters, unlike sons, are expected to be docile, dutiful, meek and simple. They are supposed to please all those surrounding them and to conform to the norms of a patriarchal society. When a daughter fails to do so, she is labelled as willful, self-centred and uncaring. Virmati who is entrapped by her own sensuality, as much as lured by the seductive promises of the professor is considered the black sheep of the family.

Caught in the whirlpool of misplaced passion towards the already married professor, she has the temerity to spurn marriage, attempts suicide and bears confinement. Sometimes she thinks about him as "a man who is already married and a traitor to his wife can never give happiness to any woman. He is a worldly person caught in his own desires" (85). She is agitated when she realizes the hopelessness of her illicit love when Ganga is pregnant for the second time. How could it be true? Man professing his love for her on one hand and making his wife pregnant on the other. At this juncture, decisively and brusquely, she cuts him saying: "you think you can do what you like so long as you go on saying you love" (110) and goes to Lahore for further studies. Harish still tries to convince her of his sincere love. He appears there stating that he would not live without her. "There is a void in my heart and in my home that you alone can fill" (112), he declares. Unable to resist his pleas further she succumbs to his requests which act eventually and lead to an abortion. Wishing to relish the fruit of education, freedom and independence, she joins as a Principal in a school at Nahan. She does not know that love and autonomy cannot coexist. Love makes one vulnerable and vulnerability does not lead to autonomy. Harish goes to Nahan also. He is adamant on not losing her:

> Arjun, what did you see when you hit the eye of the bird with the arrow, the eye that all your brothers missed? Guruji, I saw nothing, just the black dot in the centre. So Harish saw nothing but Virmati. A flying arrow aimed at a still bird. (171)

Not giving a moment's thought to how his visits to Nahan affect Virmati's life, Harish goes there also. It can be easily understood, what type of scandals these visits to a single and unmarried woman may evoke. They cost her, her job. Once again her identity as a respectable woman, 'a good daughter' is at stake.

The novelist portrays the real attitude of the professor who intellectually enjoys the best of the two worlds. His wife Ganga attends him as a maidservant, fulfils his everyday needs, and keeps his house tidy and his clothes washed and Virmati satisfies his academic urge. To study man-woman relationship, Germaine Greer, uses the analogy of employer and employee and calls women "life-contracted unpaid workers" (Greer 329) who cannot expect liberation "unless individual women agree to be outcasts, eccentrics, perverts and whatever the power- that- be choose to call them" (Greer 328). She tells women that "to be emancipated from the helplessness and walk freely upon the earth that is your birthright" (Greer 330).

Harish is very unethical and insincere in nature. He expects his wife to do all the household tasks assigned to her and to show genuine interest in the areas of his interest. At the same time he does not even recognize the work his wife does:

> How would she ever to dream that without the desire to read and write, she was going defenseless into union with a man so unlike the others she knew, who did not seem to care about her household skills at all? Yet he was impatient and angry when food was badly cooked and the house carelessly managed. The woman sighed... (37)

He is very insensible towards his wife Ganga who is "exemplary, thrifty, efficient, industrious and respectful" (210) according to his mother. As this poor woman cannot fulfil all his desires, he even goes to the extent of marrying Virmati, without considering the fact that he should be faithful to his wife. But, belonging to a subordinate creed, can his wife even dream of doing the same to him because he does not share her simple pleasures? She can only lament for her fate. At any cost Ganga's sufferings, caused by Harish's nature, should not be overlooked. Simone de Beauvoir very effectively brings out the unfortunate state of women in marriage:

> It is the duplicity of the husband that dooms the wife to a misfortune of which he complains later that he is himself the victim. Just as he wants her to be at once warm and cool in bed, he requires her to be wholly his and yet no burden; he wishes her to establish him in a fixed place on earth and to leave him free, to assume the monotonous daily round and not to bore him, to be always at hand and never importunate; he wants to have her all

> to himself and not to belong to her; to live as one of the couple and to remain alone. Thus she is betrayed from the day he marries her. (Beauvoir 497)

Virmati in course of time finds herself to be inapt and inadequate and memories of the stolen moments she shared with professor leave her not concentrating on the issues being spoken about. Understanding her mind, Swarnalata makes an attempt to make her realize how she is wasting her life in mistrusted relationship. She says:

> Marriage is not the only thing in life, Viru. The war, the Satyagraha movements because of all these things women are coming out of their houses-taking jobs, fighting, and going to jail- wake up from your stale dream. (139)

The novelist has portrayed the protagonist as a woman caught in the conflict between the passions of the flesh and a yearning to be a part of the political and intellectual movements of the day. Under the shade of a friend Swarnalata, Virmati attempts to analyze the communal tension involved during the Indian freedom struggle. As Gurpyari Jandial aptly writes:

> With Swaranalata, Virmati attends the Punjab Women Student's Conference. Here she seems and hears women who exude confidence and strength. She listens to them as they explain the meaning of the flag, the importance of freedom for the development of human spirit, impact of war, human right, strikes, academic freedom, rural upliftment, language etc. (Jandial 96)

Virmati blooms into a New Woman where she displays marvelous strength of mind in overcoming her dejection. She is "strong to bear the pain, silently, without anyone knowing" (101). Defying patriarchal notions that enforce a woman towards domesticity, she asserts her individuality and aspires self-reliance through education. She is not a silent rebel but is bold, outspoken, determined and action-oriented. The determined and unperturbed manner in which she burns the professor's letters shows her resolution to close the chapter and look forward to a meaningful life in Lahore.

But does Virmati blossom into a New Woman in the real sense of the term? No, inspite of her initial revolt against the family and the firm stand against the professor, she succumbs to his implorations and passions in Lahore where she goes to continue her future studies. "Loss of virginity pricks her conscience but then she overcomes the guilt by rationalizing it as outmoded morality" (114). She comes to Lahore to broaden her horizons but instead she gets involved in a useless love affair and unwed pregnancy, which makes her grow stale. The initial tenacious and assertive self gradually wanes away. She says in helplessness:

> ...as for me, I know, I have failed in my duty and I will be punished one day. Nobody can escape from their *Karma*. May be what is happening to me is part of it, and there is no use protesting. (84-85)

She understands her position and meaninglessness of her activities she is being involved with. Her emotional dependence on the professor constantly evades the question of marriage, stops her from doing anything that he disapproves. She wants to spread her wings like Swarnalata, her roommate, who is committed to meaningful activities related to freedom movement and women's emancipation. "May be I could be like Swarna from the inside secretly" (124). She thinks about her own love while her entire Nation is entrapped by the fret and fever of freedom struggle. At the Punjab Women Student's Conference, she is amazed at "how large an area of life women wanted to appropriate for themselves" (132). But these larger spaces are not for her. She wastes her time awaiting the furtive meetings with the Professor inspite of the awareness that there were "myriad instances of where she felt she had been weak or wronged" (129). She is being used and the Professor wants to have the cake and eat it too. He enjoys the best of the two worlds and is not there even at the most crucial time when she undergoes termination of pregnancy. Even afterwards when the Professor eventually marries her very reluctantly, she is given a pariah status and faces exclusion from hearth etc. which is the sole domain of the Professor's first wife, Ganga. Though she dares to cross one patriarchal threshold, she is seen caught into another where her free spirit is curbed and all she does is "adjust, compromise and adapt" (Malik, 135). In fact Virmati wants to carve a life for herself, to some extent. Again, to quote Seema Malik's observation:

> ...to some extent she even conveys a personal vision of womanhood by violating current social codes yet she lacks confidence, self-control, and farsightedness and is physically imprisoned with an underlying need to be emotionally and intellectually dependent on a superior force. (Malik 135)

Virmati lives in a cramped space and is forced into submissions though in a very subtle manner as Jaidev observes:

> Indeed, any sophisticated structure today functions not by direct, visible exploitation but by making the victims willingly, freely, and happily give in to its imperative. (Jaidev 57)

Professor Harish's attitude towards her is patronizing and demeaning. His interest in her is an extension of self-love-awakening her intellect and emotions inflate his ego. Undergoing a gradual process of self-effacement, her energies are directed towards pleasing him while she herself remains parched. Kapur has brought out how male ego-centricism blinds men to the situation of women, who may be placed in agonizing circumstances on account of their relationship with men. She finds her status as a second wife problematic owing to the antagonism of family members. She remains a social misfit, as contemporary social ethos does not approve of such an alliance. At her married home, the mother-in law feels she is a woman who "strayed", the stepson calls her "a gandi (bad) mummy" (208).

Her mind and her heart are constantly agitated, rippled and tumultuous with thoughts of her freedom and position in the society and family. All the time she feels left out and unwanted. This is because from washing his clothes to polishing his shoes, to tidying his desk, dusting his precious books, filling his fountain pens with ink, putting his records back in the jackets, mending his clothes, hemming his dhotis, seeing that they are properly starched, Ganga, the first wife does it all. Observing all this, the questions regarding her own peripheral existence crisscross her mind, as the novelist writes her mind in the following words: "And what about her? What kind of wife was she going to be if everything was to be done by Ganga?" (216).

For Virmati the days keep passing, empty like the day before. She tries to become friendly with Guddiya, her sister-in-law but she pretends to be busy with her homework and other household works. Manju Kapur oppositely projects her position in the family as "though not overtly hostile, in the warring factions that existed in the house, she belonged to the opposition side" (219). On her arrival in Amritsar, she writes and tells her own family that she is married but nobody comes to see her. Not even the young ones to whom she has practically been a mother. She realizes that she has transgressed. However, one day she decides to make amends and pays visit home with this feeling in her heart. The novelist describes her movement: "Full of desperate hope, Road. Virmati shuffled down Lapel Griffin road" (220). All blood relations seem cold and barren. Nobody wants her, nobody likes her. They are certainly contorted with rage and implacably hostile. When she reaches home she does not dare to enter into the house from the front door. However, she does from the backyard, where the cows are kept. It is very symbolic, the very core member of the family loses the right to enter into the house unhesitatingly. Moreover when her mother happens to see her standing there, she hurls all possible harsh words and asks her to get out of the house:

> You've destroyed our family you badmash! ...You have blackened our face everywhere! For this I gave you birth? Because of you there is shame on me, shame on Bade Pitaji! But what do you care, brazen that you are! (221)

Virmati's false hopes are finally shattered. She realizes that all ties between herself and her family are broken. Despite all care and concern, all sacrifice and responsibility that she carried out being the daughter of the family, they have flung her away. She feels wretched and lacerated and remains aloof and unattended. That is the reason when Harish takes pride in discussing the political scenario at national and international level; she is worried about her own freedom. Harish tells Virmati:

> Now it's our turn next. Now they will have no excuse. Cripps had given a commitment. At the San Francisco Peace Conference the eyes of the world will be on Britain. There will be pressure put on her recognize our sovereignty... No, Britain is now finished, Viru, finished. (254-55)

She does not respond to the above statement coming from Harish's lips, but she thinks herself:

> And me, thought Virmati, what about me? The war, or the end of it.... Suddenly he is transformed. He becomes visionary.... I feel so utterly left out, so utterly cold. Will there be any change in my life, I wonder? (255)

She rather starts delving deep into herself. She wants

her needs to be acknowledged. This is the reason when she refuses to go back home and she tells herself bluntly:

> I will relate to you with dignity or not at all. None of this hiding and whispering and keeping my voice down and struggle over who is going to wash your underwear and who is going to clean your shoes. None of this for me. (155-56)

The marital home and bed that she seems to have craved for years, she is ready to renounce and look for an opening. In another incident we can easily envisage her struggle clearly, when Virmati gives birth to a girl, she suggests "Bharti" as a name, since she feels that God had blessed her with the child at the dawn of freedom of the country but this is out-rightly rejected by Harish and he names the child as "Ida" which sounds as a Persion name to Virmati. Over this, Harish irritatingly remarks: "Let anybody think what they like for us it means a new slate and a blank beginning" (277).

Apart from narrating how Harish's irrational ideas and Virmati's irrevocable mistake divide two families. This novel also reveals the attitude of three generations of women- Kasturi, Virmati's mother, Virmati and Ida, Virmati's daughter. It captures the complex relationship between the mothers and the daughters over a tenure of three generations.

Virmati's rebellious attitude against her mother is a consequence of her mother's tendency of ignoring her. At times Virmati yearns for affection; for some sigh that she is special. Kasturi's relation with Virmati does not let her realize her daughter's need for a separate identity, an independent existence. So, Virmati has to rebel. She has to fight against the power of the mother as well as the oppressive forces of patriarchy symbolized by the mother figure.

In trying not being like her mother, and to portray herself as the key negative of her mother, Ida confirms the centrality of Virmati, from which she can have no escape. It brings out Virmati's positive stature in the novel. Ida not only questions the centre/periphery, positive/negative dualism but reconstructs the story of her mother's life by allowing her imagination to follow:

> In searching for a woman I could know, I have pieced together material from memories that were muddled, partial and contradictory. The places I visited, the stuff I read tantalized me with fragments that I knew...did. All through, I felt the excitement of discovery, the pleasure of fitting narratives into a discernible inheritance. (258)

Ida, thus becomes as much the creator of Virmati, as the latter is of Ida. But her creation is of a different sort. She transgresses "biology" to create with her mind, her intellect. She rejects her traditional association with "nature" as a woman and embraces the world of "culture".

It is possible to trace the feminism implicit in the novel through Ida's impatience towards her mother's weaknesses. When her Parvati Masi says that Virmati was a simple girl at heart, Ida says: "I hate the word 'simple'. Nobody has any business to live in the world and know nothing about its ways" (207). No woman, who dares to spurn patriarchal protection can afford to be ignorant, simple or naive? Surely, Virmati's unwed pregnancy and then its heartless termination is unpalatable to Ida who finally breaks up with her husband, Prabhakar because he forces her to have an abortion: "In denying that incipient little thing in my belly, he sowed the seeds of our breakup". (144) And then, does passion so transform an individual that Virmati fails to see things in the right perspective? She not only disregards her filial duty but also becomes a victimizer by usurping what rightfully belongs to Ganga, the Professor's first wife, thereby giving a setback to the much-needed feeling of sisterhood among women. The concluding lines of the novel reiterate Ida's rejection of Virmati, not as a mother but as a woman:

> This book weaves a connection between my mother and me, each word a brick in a mansion I made with my head and my heart. Now live in it, Mama, and leave me. Do not haunt me any more. (258)

Ida, who grows up struggling to be the "model daughter" does not have the heart to reject Virmati, the mother, but her head, the rationale, rejects her as a woman after having an insight into her past.

Through Ida's admiration for Swarnlata, who enters into a wider socio-political sphere, the novelist seems to be saying that a woman can maintain her individuality and pursue her interest without threatening the family structures. Thus, a woman should basically strive towards a fine interdependent partnership. But if she feels suffocated, then voice ought to be raised and there should be a total breaking away, like Ida. But merely transcending societal norms is not enough. A woman should be aware, self-controlled, strong-willed, self-reliant and rational, having the inner strength of womanhood. A meaningful change can be brought only from within by being free in the deeper psychic sense.

The novel projects the belief that the mother is the central figure in one's life. As an individual, she may not be very important but her presence seems to be important for both physical and psychological growth of the daughters. In the novel all the daughters, from time to time, experience despair, as they feel trapped by an oppressive environment but living in their own sheltered and limited existence, the mothers turn a blind eye to their daughter's needs. The free unconditional love that the daughter wants from her mother does not seem to exist. If Kasturi as a mother is truly disappointing, Virmati is a complete failure. The girl who proves to be a caring mother figure to her youngest sibling, Paro, is unable to extend that same loving care to her own daughter, Ida. The conservative mother, who is remembered by her daughter as "silent, brisk and bad tampered" (2) is far removed from the rebel daughter who stands in her old faded picture with a wistful melancholic beauty about her. The only memories which Ida has of her childhood reveal the struggle she had to go through to become the "model daughter" that her parents wanted her to be. As she recalls:

> Pressure, pressure to perform day and night.... My mother tightened her reins on me as I grew older. She said it was for my own good. As a result, I am constantly looking for escape routes. (258)

Manju Kapur's novel, by exploring the multi-dimensional relationship between mothers-daughters, clearly imparts the message that unfulfilled mothers cannot offer fulfillment to their daughters. For a healthy, nurturing relationship between the two, it is necessary for women to be enlightened as well as liberated. As Simone de Beauvoir rightly points out:

> The mother's relation with her children takes from within the totality of her life, it depends upon her relation with her husband, her past, her occupation, herself. (Beauvoir 537)

These three generations of women represent the attitudinal changes with the passage of time. Kasturi represents complete acceptance, Virmati- adjustments and Ida- complete non-adjustment. Kasturi completely belongs to the traditional times where women employment is unheard totally, hence complete acceptance and subordination to men are expected from them. She has no complaints against her life or against her husband because she has no expectations. Ida completely belongs to the recent times where the sight of highly educated and employed women is very common. Virmati is in the transition phase, hence compromising and conflicting.

It is not clear whether Kasturi, who is safe in the net of traditional value system, or Virmati, who is in the transition phase, or Ida, completely liberated are really happy with their lives. The crux of the point is only that women have become some what modernized. Men refuse to do so because they know it that becoming modern is to lose their position and status in the society and to accept woman as their equal in all aspects. But in the guise of being modernized, men have detected other means to exploit women. Until this attitude is changed; there will not be real harmony between man and woman. Only then, we can realize the concept of *Ardhanaareeswara*- the ideal state of man-woman relationship- which emphasizes that man and woman are not opposites but complementary to each other.

In the traditional social milieu of the novel, where these mothers and daughters exist, marriage is regarded as the ultimate goal and destiny from which they cannot escape. They want their daughters to be "good girls" and "properly married". In this regard, Simone de Beauvoir says:

> A generous mother, who sincerely seeks her child's welfare, will as a rule think that it is wiser to make a "true woman" of her, since society will more readily accept her if this is done. (Beauvoir 309)

Although the only thing which Kasturi has got from her marriage is poor health and children, yet to get her daughters married seems to be the only concern of her life. According to her: "It is the duty of every girl to get married" (13) and she tells Virmati that "a woman without her own home and family is a woman without moorings" (102). Ida, remembers her mother telling her a number of times that she would be "lucky" if she found a husband like her father. Shakuntala's mother Lajwanti is frustrated to "have an unmarried daughter nearing thirty was a fate so devastating that it must excuse any loss of temper" (147). Ironically, the only expression of motherly care is extended in the form of "home- made sheets of fine Manchester cotton or embroidered pillow cases, brightly woven Kheses" (61) that Kasturi's mother prepares for her daughter to take after marriage to her own home. The same is done by Kasturi for Virmati, but her refusal to marry the boy of her mother's choice, the precious rewards of affection from her mother are bestowed upon the second daughter, Indumati. Manju Kapur's novel breaks the myth of the mother as a "nurturing and fear-dispelling presence" (Kakkar 83). Rather than being a source of comfort, the mother figure emerges as an unsympathetic, threatening force in the daughter's life. Restricting, demanding, nagging- it is she who, more than anyone else, sows the seeds of difficulty in the path of her daughter by refusing to acknowledge her needs, aspirations and longings, and withholding from her the protection and understanding that the daughter desperately seeks. Discussing the mother-daughter relationship, Simone de Beauvoir observes:

> The daughter is for the mother at once her double and another person, the mother is at once overweeningly affectionate and hostile towards her daughter: she saddles her child with her own destiny: a way of revenging herself for it. (Beauvoir 309)

In other words, a daughter is an alter ego of her mother. The mother wants to realize her unfulfilled dreams through her daughter.

The mothers train their daughters to become exemplary daughters-in law, just like Kasturi, or Ganga. The advice given to Ganga by her mother-in law, Kishori Devi, holds true for all the young women, be they a daughter or a daughter-in law:

> In this life we can do nothing but our duty, serve our elders, our children, walk along the path that has been marked for us, and not pine and yearn for those things we cannot have. (194)

Virmati whose desire to escape the hostile environment at home leads her into the humiliating compromise to become the second wife of the Professor, also decides to "walk tight-lipped, mute, on the path her destiny had created out for her" (196) and is remembered by her daughter as a woman who never asserted herself after her marriage. As Ida says firmly:

> She couldn't have, because when I grew up I was very careful to tailor my needs to what I knew I could get. That is my female inheritance. That is what she tried to give me. Adjust, compromise, adapt. (236)

The three words which govern not only Ida's life but also that of Kasturi, Virmati, Ganga, her daughter Chotti and all the women in the male-oriented society.

Manju Kapur, in her novel does not provide solutions to the problems faced by these women. She only raises questions like, Is woman's need for liberation opposed to tradition? Why is education inadequate to create a better environment for women? Or why do women help in alienating and subjugating the members of their own sex? Though there are no easy solutions, it is only women who can find answers to these questions. Liberation has to come from within, as women have to believe in their inner strength and get rid of their insecurities, deep-rooted prejudices and dogmas, which compel them to propagate the unfair rules of a male-dominated society. Betty Friedan accuses society of considering "identity crisis" as man's problem only. "The crises of growing up, of choosing his identity, the decision as to what one is and is going to be" (Friedan 68) are considered only male prerogatives, and women are told that "truly feminine women do not want careers, higher education, political rights, the independence and the opportunities" (Friedan 13). Once women come together with the right perspective and achieve the required harmony and balance in their lives, there will be no stopping them.

Virmati struggles through the winds of misfortune in her love for the Professor. She has a constant longing for self autonomy but her search for freedom is otherwise proved to be self-deceptive horrendous and meaningless. There is an unresolved dichotomy in the character portrayal of Virmati, the female protagonist. While she is strong willed to resist all kinds of social and family pressures, she is not strong enough to stay away from the Professor's influence. Perhaps, lack of maternal love and loss of familial affection explain the protagonist's weakness. Virmati needs love and an identity; she misses it. The Professor symbolizes the only hope of fulfilling this need and achieving the desired identity. It can be possible that Virmati is in love with the concept of love rather than with person viz. Professor Harish. Thus, Virmati is an example of feminine suffering. This suffering is also largely due to the individual awareness in a conservative community, becoming an outcaste in the family, as if in exile, due to a woman's rejection of the mythical model of an ideal daughter but the only satisfaction she has in her life is that she has lived a life of her choice.

Difficult Daughters represents the turmoil of a woman who tries to overcome her cultural identity and forge a self-identity, an attempt which leaves a woman hard hearted, and desolate. I think the author is very much inclined to say that however educated or innovative an Indian woman is, her Indian background and psyche cannot feel gratified unless society approves of her endeavours and her relationship. Virmati's tragedy is the tragedy of ambition, obsession and un-acclaimed ovation. Thus, Manju Kapur's *Difficult Daughters* is a feminist discourse not because she is a woman writing about woman but because she "has understood a woman both as a woman and as a person pressurized by all kinds of visible and invisible contexts" (Jaidev, 68). She presents feminism at its most sane, keeping in mind the Indian context.

Works Cited

Beauvoir, Simone de. *The Second Sex*. Harmondsworth: Penguin, 1983.

Das, Veena. *Critical Events: An Anthropological Perspective in Contemporary Indian Writers.* New Delhi: O. U. P., 1995.

Friedan, Betty. *The Feminine Mystique.* Harmondsworth: Penguin, 1965.

Greer, Germaine. *The Female Eunuch.* St. Albana: Paladin, 1976.

Jaidev. "Problematizing Feminism." *Gender and Literature,* ed. Iqbal Kaur. New Delhi: B. R. Publishers, 1992.

Jandial, Gur Pyari. "Manju Kapur's Difficult Daughters: A Study in Transition from Chaos to Integration." *The Commonwealth Review,* Vol. 12 No. 1, 2000-01.

Kakkar, Sudhir. *The Inner World.* New Delhi: O.U.P., 1978.

Kapur, Manju. *Difficult Daughters.* New Delhi: Penguin India, 1998; London: Faber and Faber, 1998.

Malik, Seema. "Partition and Women Writers: A Reading of Anita Kumar's *The Night of the Seven Dawns,* Mehr Nigar Masroor's *Shadows of Time* and Shauna Singh Baldwin's *What the Body Remembers.*" *Discussing Indian Women Writers: Some Feminist Issues,* eds. R. K. Dhawan and Alessandro Monti. New Delhi: Prestige, 2002.

Mitchell, Juliet. "Women and Equality." *The Rights and Wrongs of Women,* eds. Juliet Mitchell and Ann Oakley. Harmondsworth: Penguin, 1976.

Singh, Veena. "How Difficult are Difficult Daughters? Sunlight on a Broken Column and Difficult Daughters as Female Bildungsroman." *Contemporary Indian Literature and Expositions,* ed. Santosh Gupta. Jaipur: Rawat Publications, 2000.

10

Women's search for identity in Manju Kapur's *Home*

Sudista Prasad Singh

Human Rights impart equal right to men and women. But women are not treated equally in the real affairs of life. They are discriminated and deprived of human rights by the society. They are discriminated from the birth to the end of their life. Though, the post-modern age has changed the old concept of women's sub-ordination and subjugation, they are still forced to be servile in spite of their ability to lead their male partners. Daughters are considered less important than sons. The mother is not considered in the family and the society unless she becomes the mother of a son. These are the cases of violation of human right to women. Many women writers have raised the voice against such discrimination and tried their best to establish the identity of women.

During the last two decades of twentieth century i.e. 1980s and 1990s, there was a spurt in feministic oulook and search for women's identity. A number of women writers came on the fore front to raise their voices against ages-old prejudiced bias of patriarchy system against women in all social and economic affairs of life. Women writers like Bharati Mukherjee, Arundhati Roy, Anita Nair, Shashi Deshpande, Anita Desai, Manju Kapur and some others are vocal exponents of women's identity and their equality in socio-economic affairs of life. They are violent in their speeches against domestic and social violence inflicted on the women who serve the family and society as mothers, wives, sisters, daughters and daughters-in-law. Though they are specially gifted with the power of creations by nature, they are subjugated and sub-ordinated in every affair of life. Manju Kapur has very clearly exposed such discriminations against women through her novel *Home* and asserted their identity.

Manju Kapur is presently the Professor of English at Miranda College in Delhi University. She has written only three novels i.e. *Difficult Daughters* (1998). *A Married Woman* (2002) and *Home* (2006). With the publication of her very first novel she became a renowned novelist, having won Commonwealth Writer's Prize for her excellence. In this novel her female protagonist Virmati turns rebellious against patriarchy system which cuts her wings of freedom and deprives her personal identity. In the second novel *A Married Woman* her female protagonist turns to lesbianism to challenge the men's superiority and women's dependence on men even for emotional fulfillment of womanhood. In her third novel *Home* Manju Kapur became rebellions against the age old prejudices which degraded woman's position in the family in comparison with the men's position that sub-jugated women and denied their identity. A woman's position in her husband's house is not secure unless she begets a male-child because she is known only as some body's daughter, wife or mother. She has no identity of her own. In the words of Sahukar and Patel:

> A childless marriage is a source of serious disappointment and sooner or later, leads to serious trouble. The position of a wife in her husband's family remains shaky and unpredictable until she

> begets a child. She becomes secure only after the birth of a male child". (Sahukar & Patel 81)

Home deals with the traditional bias against women in the patriarchy system of our society. It is the story of a joint family headed by Banwari Lal, a resident of Karol Bagh in New Delhi. Sona and Rupa are two sisters. Sona is married to Yashpal, the eldest son of Banbari Lal. She performs religious rituals and prayers but remains childless for ten years after her marriage so, she is humiliated by the family members and relatives. After continuous struggle for ten years, she gives birth to a daughter, Nisha but her task is not fulfilled until she gives birth to a son. Now she is the mother of a child but a female child. So her status of motherhood is not considered as important as the mother of a son. She prays to God for a son and her prayer is considered. Ultimately she is blessed with a son. Though she gives birth to a son through a big "caesarian" process, she experiences to be the most blessed woman. She feels that her sad days of disgrace and resentment are gone for ever with the birth of her little son, Raju: "Gone was the disgrace, the resentment, gone with the appearance of little Raju, as dark pain - featured as his father, but a boy, a boy". (49)

Sona experiences the bitterness of mother without a son in Indian patriarchal society but she does not mend her mind. She deals with the same prejudiced views of Indian mother-in- law who faces the problem of personal identity if they don't become the mother of sons. When Pooja, Sona's daughter- in- law becomes the mother of a daughter, Sona wants that "she (Pooja) should try two or three times for boy".

Indian women are conniving with other women. They do not like to cooperate other women in search of their identity. Rupa Bajwa in her "Sari Shop" has very clearly explained such idiosyncrasies of women in her novel. Anita Desai also accepts it and tells that women "connive at patriarchal morals". All over the world, women are rebellions against patriarchal prejudices which allow them to have equal status in the society. They are subjugated and forced to follow the dictates of traditional society. They are compelled to be meek, docile and passive workers of the family.

Shashi Deshpande turns rebellions in her novels against such discriminatory and biased attitude of patriarchal system of society in which code of conduct is imposed on women. They can't search for their personal identity. Deshpande exposes it through Indu - the protagonist of her novel *Roots and Shadows*:

> I must be obedient and unquestioning. As a girl they told me I must be meek and submissive. Why? I had asked. Because you are female. (Deshpande 58)

The same idea is repeated in *Home* when Nisha comes to her in-law's house after marriage. She touches the feet of her mother-in-law and moves into the kitchen to see the arrangement of the kitchen. Her mother suggests her that household is the main affair of the girls and education is meant for boys and male members only: "What does a girl need with studying? Cooking will be useful for entire life" (206). In her father's home also every member of the family even her mother and brothers impose code of conduct an women.

Both Pooja and Nisha, the daughter and daughter- in-law of Sona face the same discrimination as faced by Sona who herself being a woman does not allow them to assert their identity. In the name of tradition and respect for patriarchal culture they are not allowed to take part in the main affairs of society. They are enclosed in the four walls of home: "Tradition and respect for culture, fondness for rules and regulations which bind society together is an amalgamating feature of this haveli. The women in the haveli are secluded from the main stream of social life, enclosed by the power barrier of the purdah". (Kumar, T 53)

The mind of Sona is colonised by male oriented power

structure of traditional society which restricts her from asserting her own identity and makes her the subject of humiliation till she becomes the mother of a son. She does not understand the power-play of male empowered society which undermines the women's identity and their freedom of choice in decision-making of any important policy-matters. In the male-dominate traditional society, every thing is determined by male members of the family and society. No space is left for women to assert their identity. KS Amish Kumar has rightly said that:

> In the male-oriented power structure, every thing is determined by the power and hence the so-called powerful males dominate the entire space and colonise the females. (113)

Women subjugation and discrimination is global phenomena. It is not limited to any particular country on continent, parents discriminate between the son and the daughter. They don't allow their daughters the same freedom as their sons. They don't make the same expenditure on the education of the daughters like their sons. Their responsibilities are finished after the marriage of daughters. They think that daughters are burden on them till they are married. They think that girls are their liabilities where as the sons are their assets, so they don't think so much for the education of daughters, like sons. Anita Desai in her novel *Fasting, Feasting* expresses the same discrimination between the son and the daughter by parents. The protagonist of the novel, Uma faces such discrimination by her parents. Her brother, Arun is sent abroad for higher education while Uma is badly engaged in domestic affairs of the family and faces scowling and scolding of her father and mother. She says, "Despite a slight variation in the roles they have chosen to play, papa's of scowling and Mama's scolding." (10)

Uma feels as an unpaid servant for her self-centred parents and finds no escape from her entrapment in her own parents' home. Rama Mehta in her novel *Inside the*

Haveli has expressed the entrapment of a daughter-in-law in her in-law's home. Geeta, the female protagonist of the novel rebels against the restrictions and her confinement inside the four walls of home.

Everywhere, we find gender disparity and discrimination which cause infringement of women's right to equality. The Booker Prize winner Arundhati Roy, in her Novel *The God of Small Things* is very critical of such gender discrimination in Indian society. Amnu, the protagonist of the novel faces the same discrimination. His brother Chacko does not allow her to be the share holder of the pickle factory established by her mother, though she works in the factory more than her brother. "Chacko says, "what's yours is mine and what's mine is also mine". (57) After divorce, she comes to her father's home where she finds no place for herself and her children.

In her novel *Home* Manju Kapur has raised a very pertinent question of women's identity. She raises the question, "Home, for whom?" Before marriage parents' home is supposed to be the daughter's home but after marriage this home becomes alien to her. In her in-law's house also she is neglected and humiliated if she does not bring rich dowry for her husband and in-laws. Her position becomes shaky till she becomes the mother of a son. Here the novelist has posed the question of women's place in home. Women must have their place in home of her parents and husband. They must have their identities in their homes where they can enjoy complete freedom like male members of the society. Kapur has decried the place of women in traditional society like the female protagonist of Sylvia Plath in her novel *Mirror*. The mirror reflects whatever comes before it. All the things are identified which come before it but the mirror has no identity. The woman who keeps the home, nurses the family and gives birth to the child who will shoulder the future responsibility of the nation, becomes homeless. She has no identity in the family except the roles assigned to her as wife, mother, daughter and daughter-in-law to cater the needs of the family. She can't go against the wishes of male counterpart in the home. Manju Kapur's *Home* ironically denotes passivity and homelessness of the woman who is mistress of the house. But she is the puppet in the hands of men in traditional society. There is nothing of her own in the home. Shashi Despandey is more rebellious to assert the identity of the woman in her novel *The Dark Holds No Terror.* The female protagonist of the novel 'Saru' finds her parents' home as "homeless refuge" and torture, humiliation and subjugation at husband's house but she does not surrender unlike Amu of *The God of Small Things* who breaks for her own identity. Saru says, "My Life is my own". She asserts her identity confronting the hard realities and becomes willing to continue her practice in medicine because doctor in her is more important to have her identity than her roles in the family.

Manju Kapur has raised a very serious question before the traditional society which restricts the woman from asserting her identity. She is not free economically and socially. She is chained from birth to death and not allowed to same freedom as her male counterpart in the family. It is injustice on the part of the woman. We cannot expect the healthy society in which the woman is forced to be servile like unpaid servant. She must have her share in the home and should not be neglected and subjugated like Sona of the novel *Home*. But women should also change their idiosyncrasies and treat their daughter's- in -law like their sons.

Works Cited

Sahukar, Pratibha Mukherjee and Patel, B.K. " But I am not a woman", *The Indian Journal of English Studies* , Vol. XLV., 2008.

Kapur , Manju. *Home*. New Delhi: Ramdom House, 2006.

Kumar, Tribhuwan. "Rama Mehta: An Epitome of Indian Feminism", *Cyber Literature,* Patna, Vol. XXII No. 11, December 2008.

Kumar, K. S. Amish. "Politicising the personal: A Feminist Reading of Margaret Alexander's Select Poems", *The Common Wealth Review,* New Delhi, Vol. XVI No -1.

Desai, Anita. *Fasting, Feesting.* London: Vintage, 1999.

Roy, Arundhati. *The God of Small Things.* New Delhi: Penguin Books, 2002.

Deshpande, Shashi. *Roots and Shadows.* New Delhi: Orient Longman, 1992.

11

Portraits of Women in Arundhati Roy's *The God of Small Things*

Sakshi Tyagi and *Sandeep Kumar*

The caste system in India is an important part of ancient Hindu tradition and dates back to 1200BC. The term caste was first used by Portuguese travellers who came to India in the16th century. Caste comes from the Spanish and Portuguese word caste which means race, breed or lineage. Many Indians use the term jati. Different castes fall under four basic Varnas:

Brahmins-Priests
Kshatryas-Warriors
Vaishyas-Traders
Shudras-Labourers

Members of high caste enjoy more wealth and opportunities while members of a low caste perform menial jobs. Outside the caste system are the untouchables. They are considered polluted and not to be touched. Untouchables have separate entrance to homes and must drink from separate wells. Untouchables were named *harijans* (children of God) by Gandhiji, while the census authorities during the British rule referred to them as Exterior Classes. Now a days they are popularly known as the depressed or *dalits*. The difficulty of living in a caste- based society, for those towards the top, and those near the bottom, is the focus of the novel, *The God of Small Things*. The novel centres around the family of the descendents of the Reverend Ipe. The family comprised of all ages and attitudes, from the twins Estha and Rahel, their mother and her brother Chacko to the strict Baby Kochamma, to Pappachi and Mammachi, as the head of the family. Arundhati Roy, a great champion of the downtrodden and the have -nots, the *dalit*, deserted, points out those unnoticed shades of a social problem which generally escapes the eyes of social scientists. The characters in Roy's novel exist in a culture of strict rules. There is a caste system and a class system that exert much force upon the characters. Conflict is created for the individuals who can't adhere to these systems of social organization and control. We come across three characters in *The God of Small Things* who belong to the category of the downtrodden. They are Vellya Pappan and his two sons Kuttapen and Velutha. They belong to an untouchable caste called *paravan*. Arundhati Roy gives a lot of information about the untouchables of Kerala in this connection. She also gives a generally perfect picture of *dalits* with their varying responses to the caste oppression through the device of trio. Vellya Paapen, Kuttapen and Velutha constitute the trio, which depicts three types of the dalits in Indian society.

Mammachi told Estha and Rahel that she could remember a time, in her girlhood, when they were expected to crawl backwards with a broom, sweeping away their footprints so that Brahmins or Syrian Christians would not defile themselves by accidentally stepping into a *paravan's* footprints. In Mammachi's time, paravans, like other untouchables were not allowed to walk on public roads, not allowed to cover their upper bodies, not allowed to carry umbrellas. They had to put their hands over their mouths when they spoke, to divert polluted breath away from those whom they addressed.

Conditions have changed since then. They use public roads. They are also learning skills other than their traditional occupations. Though that does not bring as much monetary gain to them as to the touchable folk. For instance, Mammachi pays Velutha more than she normally does to a *paravan* but less than that to a touchable. Neither the orthodox Mammachi nor the progressive Pillai permits them to step inside their houses. The untouchables are becoming members of the Communist party and trade unions and marching along with others in processions wearing shirts. They are introduced to the idea of equal rights but we are also informed that touchable workers grudge their equal rights. Chacko as the factory owner wants to prevent the growth of real trade union led by Velutha in his factory. Pillai finds a threat to his ambitions in Velutha as the latter's working class background seems a plus point in the race for party and trade union leadership. It is remarkable to note that the institution of untouchablity has not left Christianity unaffected. Even the Communists in the pursuit of immediate electoral gains submit to it.

Vellya Paapen, the oldest of the three untouchables in the novel is an 'old world paravan' as the novelist puts it. Born and brought up in the age when *paravans* had to crawl backward he takes for granted the social disabilities imposed on the untouchables by tradition. He dares not question or violate the caste rules. Obviously he believes that it will be sinful to deviate from that and makes him a defender of social status quo, a zealous guardian of conformity, highly fearful of change. With his deep rooted faith in tradition, Vellya fears for his younger son and resents the way he says, the way he does. Strangely enough his concern anticipates the complaint of Baby Kochamma to the police:

> She described to inspector Thomas Mathew how

> it was not just what velutha had said that had made her to come but the way he said it. (260-261)

Vellya Paapen has a gratitude to Mammachi and her family. Reverend John Ipe gave Vellya's father, ken land title to the land on which his hut now stands. Then when Vellya had an accident and lost one of his eyes, Mammachi paid for his glass eye. Of course, it was paid as a loan but Vellya has not been able to work off his debt nor seems to be able to do that ever. He is also grateful to Mammachi for she arranged Velutha's education and gave him a job. That Mammchi and her family too have been benefited from their labour. So when he comes to know of what his son has done, he feels obliged to go to Mammachi to report. He weeps and trembles and offers to return his mortgaged eye. His son and Mammchi's daughter have made "the unthinkable thinkable and the impossible really happen" . (256) Mammchi does not at first believe him and pushes him with all her strength. He falls down. While she continues calling him names like "drunken dog" and "drunken paravan liar". (255-256) It is only Baby Kochamma who takes it as credible.

In the conflict between loyalty and love, the former gains the upper hand. As the novelist remarks:

> By the time he understood his part in history's plans, it was too late to retrace his steps. He had swept his footprints away himself. Crawling backward with a broom. (200)

Kuttapen is the elder son of Vellya Paapen who lives with his father and younger brother. He pursues traditional jobs of his caste until he becomes disabled. Kuttapen is a good as well as safe paravan because he cannot read or write that is, though there are schools for untouchables, but people in power prefer to keep them illiterate because that is less likely to awaken their social consciousness. Ignorant people are less able to protest and defy than the awakened.

Velutha, the younger son of Vellya Paapen is not a conformist like his father and elder brother. He is not and cannot become a 'laltain' needing oil from outside. He is a 'mombatti' (candle) burning by himself. He is self illumined and self- confident and has got the self esteem, the qualities which make a man remarkable.

Veltha's name is rather ironical because the word means white in Malayalam but his complexion is black. This conflict between the names really seems to be indicative of other conflict in the novel of the same type. This untouchable master craftsman floats on the periphery of society yearning to be accepted, confident and recognized like O'Neill's black protagonist, Yank in *The Hairy Ape*. Velutha is about three years younger than Ammu. He is not illiterate like his father and elder brother because when he was about eleven, Mammachi noticed his natural skills and persuaded his father to send him to the untouchable's school. He has learned carpentry from a German carpenter Johann Klein and knows a lot about machines. Mammachi often said that if only he hadn't been a paravan, he might have become an engineer. Velutha has served Mammachi and Chacko well both their house and at the factory. It is ironical, however, that his remuneration does not correspond to this praise and his abilities are not duly rewarded. To his employers and even to his party leaders he remains only a paravan.

Soon after the return of Velutha to Ayemenem we find him marching with a red flag in his hand and a white shirt on his body in a procession led by the Travancore-Cochin Marxist labour union. He is recognized by Rahel, though Ammu and Estha do not want to admit that in the presence of Baby Kochamma and Chacko. Baby Kochamma is humiliated by procession but she finds an easy target for her wrath which is transferred against Velutha. Ammu knows Velutha from his boyhood days. He made intricate toys for Ammu and brought them to her. Though he was younger than Ammu, he used to call her Ammukutty (little Ammu). The procession event leads a happy discovery of kindred rebellious spirit in Velutha. She hopes that "under his careful cloak of cheerfulness, he housed a living, breathing anger against the smug, ordered world that she so raged against." (176) Besides the kindred spirit, she finds other qualities in Velutha. Velutha's love for children is one of the factors. Of course, there is a physical aspect of the attraction too as:

> ...she wondered at how his body had changed – so quietly, from a flat muscled boy's body into a man's body...A swimmer's body. A swimmer carpenters 's body... (174-175)

Velutha too, discovers the woman in Ammu:

> ...she had deep dimples when she smiled and they stayed on long after her smile left her eyes. He saw that her brown arms were round and firm and perfect...he saw too that he was not necessarily the only giver of gifts. That she had gifts to give him too. (176)

That is how the giving and taking of gifts begin, how the mother loves the man at night that the children love in the day. The rendezvous continues for thirteen nights and then events take an unexpected turn. Velutha's father sees night after night a little boat rowed across the river and returning at dawn.

So he goes to Mammachi and tells her about a man and woman, who used to stand together in Skin to skin. That provides a golden opportunity to Baby Kochamma to settle her accounts. "She saw it as god's way of punishing Ammu for her sins and simultaneously avenging her Baby Kochamma's humiliation at the hands of Velutha and the men in the march ... "(273) She goes to the Kottayam police station and cooks up a case of attempted rape of Ammu and kidnapping of three children, one of them found dead.

As for Mammachi, she is hardly better in her behaviour to Velutha. She summons Velutha to her house and when he comes unsuspecting, she uses abusive language that surprises all the listeners. She is a sophisticated lady of ill temper who spits in the face of Velutha. Now Velutha goes to comrade Pillai, unaware of the fact that the leader considered him "the only snag". (121) Velutha is also ignorant of Pillai's advice to remove Velutha somehow, an advice that surprised Chacko. So when the naive fellow goes to Pillai, he dismisses him with the remark: "but comrade you should know that party was not constituted to support workers indiscipline in their private life. (287) At the Kattayam police station Pillai does not try to challenge false accusation against Velutha and hides the fact that he is a card - holding member of the protection of the party. He ensures his end. But there is nothing unusual or unexpected in it. He lives in a society "where a man's death could be more profitable than his life had ever been". (281)

So a procession of touchable policemen crossed the Meenachal River. They were servants of the state pledged to the virtues of politeness, obedience, loyalty, intelligence, courtesy and efficiency. They woke up Velutha with their boots and beat him severely. Rahel and Estha who were hidden in the same house woke up by the screams and came to know what had happened. Velutha had become semi- conscious and was not moving.

"His skull was fractured in three places. His nose and both his cheek-bones were smashed, leaving his face pulpy, undefined... his spine was damaged in two places the concussion had paralyzed his right arm and resulted in a loss of control over his bladder and rectum. Both his knees were shattered." (304)

Still, they brought handcuffs and locked his arms across his back. But they did not fail to make fun of his painted nail before that and one of them flicked at his penis with his stick. As he could not walk, they dragged him to the police station where he died at night.

It is remarkable to note that here Roy's portrayal of the piteous plight of the defeceless and marginalized is very near to that of Mulk Raj Anand's *Untouchable*. Mr. Anand has given birth to a character, Bakha, the hero of the novel, an untouchable who receives tyranny and injustice, insult and humiliation, sometimes on trifles and sometimes without any cause. Once Bakha inadvertently touches a Hindu in the market, the higher caste men begin to blow hot and cold and hurl at him. Bakha apologizes, implores and entreats but in vain. It is the Muslim tongawallah who comes to his rescue.

Thus, we see that *The God of Small Things* makes a scathing attack on the patriarchal notions of 'touchable' society, the high caste Hindus and their hypocrisy, ostentation and cruelty. It presents a realistic view of the caste and class system prevailing in contemporary society. It presents the true picture of *dalits* and deserted; their tireless efforts to seek an identity in an absolutely cruel and callous society; their inner defending attitudes against the surge of storm of hypocrisy and artificiality.

The book thus symbolically gives a detailed picture of life and society in their cultural pattern. It shows willful blending of rules in the worlds of small and big things, which make the life of 'mombatties' miserable. The novelist has boldly exposed the dark aspect of the patriarchal domination of a traditional society and it seems as if she has given her tacit support to 'mombatti's' struggle against caste and class structure of society.

Works Cited

Ali, Syed Mashkor, (Ed). *Indian Writing in English: A critical Response*. New Delhi: Creative Books, 2001.

Dupler, Duglas. *Critical Essay on The God of Small Things in Novels For Students*. Farmington Hills, Michigan, United States: Thomson Gale, 2006.

Roy, Amitabh. *The God of Small Things: A Novel of Social Commitment*. New Delhi: Atlantic Publishers, 2005.

Roy, Arundhati. *The God of Small Things*. London: Flamingo, 1998.

12

Shobha De's Feminism: A Brief Survey of Her Novels

Pankaj Kumar 'Niraj'

Indian fiction in English, after establishing its foothold in commonwealth literature, is now producing third generation novelists. We are progressing on to the twenty-first century. We witness the rapid changes in the social, cultural and moral norms of the society. The writers of the post-independence fiction have focussed on contemporary problems. They have explored the vital areas of individual consciousness and have projected the fascinating images of cultural change, rather transformation. Shobha De, who started her career as a journalist in 1970, has emerged on the literary scene of Indian fiction dealing with the vital aspects of existence and survival in high class society of India. Her works have no existential and psychological bearing.

Closely acquainted with the Bombay cinema and the world of Modelling, she has beautifully mirrored the shattering human values of this glittering society. Her novels occupy themselves with the themes of over-powering materialism, lack of spirituality and the resulting inner conflict, the lack of identity of women and the crumbling moral values. Her women characters represent a true picture of the modern Indian women.

Women in the male-dominated Indian society suffer a lot because of gender abuse. Denied of separate space, the women can't lead life according to feminine perspectives. The social role and position of the women are strictly assigned by patriarchal supremacy. Women are measured with the yardstick of phallocentric ideologies. Judging women as the ultimate object of male subjectivity, the male dominating society aims at curbing the female sect off their individuality and rendering them passive, subordinate roles throughout their lives. On the basis of gender discrimination, the women characters of Shobha De experience psychological and emotional trauma right from their childhood-onwards. The patriarchal parents play a vital role in suppressing the individuality of the girl children. They are forced to regimentation throughout their lives. The prevailing phallocentric ideologies create a hostile atmosphere for Shobha De's female creations and so they remain sensitive to female subordination.

Most of De's books are best sellers as she truthfully projects the image of the upper class women of contemporary India. Shobha De is a woman with multifaceted personality. The modern Indian women novelists in English Anita Desai, Shashi Deshpande, Arundhati Roy, Manju Kapur and Meena Alexander have made their permanent mark in the field of English fiction. In their writings they have tried to free the women from the age long control of male domination. In the words of Kamali:

> A woman is a writer who writes about woman as a woman.... Their writing comes out of their consciousness of the conflict between their idea of themselves as human beings and the idea that society has of them as women. All this makes their writing very clearly women's writing. (132)

The Modern Indian women, born in post-war

generation in an atmosphere of bewilderment and confusion have become bold and capable of surviving in degrading moral values of lie. These characters suffer a humiliation as far as their social economical cultural life is concerned but they also find themselves capable of struggling, compromising and realizing their existence in the end. Shobha De has very realistically presented her women strong in character, who take bold decisions to survive in society. Amar Nath Prasad observes that:

> Shobha De's novels show the novelist's perceptive portrayal of the secret depths of the human psyche;..... her saucy racy and captivating style invokes vivid images and compels the reader to identify himself or herself with the characters and situations. In short, Shobha De has tried her best to expose the moral and spiritual breakdown of modern society in which a hapless and forsaken woman longs for pleasure and wants to fly freely in the sky of freedom. (1-18)

The search for identity has been a popular theme in fiction. Many writers have portrayed the problem of the place of woman in society, her true belonging and her place in marital relationship. But, often the novels end where these problems begin; writers, no doubt, raise the problems without offering and solution. Sometimes there is an escape from the misery of the world, sometimes they yield to sorrows of the world. Paul rightly observes:

> The modern Indian woman, who is at the centre of fiction of Shobha De is no longer a model of vadic or pre-vadic dignified woman, nor is she modelled on the post-Aryan woman who is passive in nature and accepts the dominance of man in society. Born in the era of Woman's lib, they are to a certain extent an extension of the woman based on mythic models from the Ramayana and the Puranas. Modelled on Sita, Savitri and Gandhari, She becomes shy, gentle as a person, pure and

> faithful as wife and selfless, loving and thoughtful as a mother. (The Indian Nation, August 3, 1997)

Attaining adulthood doesn't free Shobha De's women from their relentless struggle against female sufferance. The women believe that by means of career, they can establish their individuality. Inexperienced and immature as they are with worldly matters, Shobha De's women like Mikki (*Sisters*) and Aasha Rani (*Starry Nights*) are forced to shoulder responsibilities in order to fulfil certain obligations. Even when the women choose their respective careers, they have no scope to achieve self-respect. They are denied the freedom to act on their own. The women undergo the pangs and pains of life due to male-superiority. As a result, De's protagonists refuse to align themselves with the prevailing patriarchal ideology. Isolated and alienated, her women characters remain traumatized. In her novels, she gives a full throated expression to the hollowness and hypocricy characterizing marriage in the Indian male-dominated societal framework. Shobha De's women characters, in spite of their revolutionary fervour towards attaining equality, are purely romantic at heart. As a result, Karuna (*Socialite Evenings*), Mikki (*Sisters*), Nisha (*Sultry Days*), Aasha Rani (*Starry Nights*) and Noor (*Snapshots*) hope for a secure marriage and a peaceful existence. On the contrary, the women are betrayed as the men turn to be selfish and money-minded opportunists who readily ditch the women at the time of crisis. Shobha De's women, therefore, refuse to align themselves with the prevailing male ideology. As Pushpalata comments:

> Men seem very passive in response to women : they are either indifferent or insensitive... Though in the Indian male-dominated society, women are marginalized by their husbands, but Shobha De's women are certainly different. They have the ability to detest the indifferent and callous attitude of the husbands who often keep themselves busy in drab

> monotonous activities like reading business pages of the newspapers. (66)

Emotionally Shattered, Shobha De's women are compelled by society to acquiesce into marriage. The women look forward towards a perspective future of equality through marriage, where their rightful decisions would be respected. Circumstances compel them to believe marriage to be a solution to all their problems. But Shobha De's women experience bitterness in conjugal life. The stereotype husbands turn to be perfect male chauvinists. In fact, they do not consider the wife to be an individual being with feelings and emotions for her own. Shobha De shows how in a phallocentric society, marriage provides the man with unquestionable power to enslave and subdue the women, thereby severing the wife off her individuality, self-respect and dignity. When Karuna (Socialite Evenings) and Mikki (Sisters) and Maya (Second Thoughts) decide to come out of the cocoon of their married life, the husbands react violently, the working women Aparna and Rashmi (Snapshots) are compelled to toil in and out without relaxation. The conflict in conjugal life leads the women to crumble down thoroughly when their earnest desire to attain motherhood is casually dismissed by the insensitive husbands, to add to the emotional sterility and mental agony. Shobha De's women have to digest the realities regarding the husband's affairs with other women as the women are disillusioned with their marital life, they remain alienated and fragmented psychologically. Shobha De's women remain lacerated due to continuous trauma that distorts their mind. The women who are compelled to seek some kind of consolation, in order to relieve their psychological tension fall into three groups. The first groups of women like Karuna (Socialite Evenings) and Maya (Second Thoughts) due to their psychological strain once again gets trapped as they choose to derive soothing comfort and temporary relief from the relationship with men outside their marriage. Their extramarital relationship in order to revolt against their insensitive husbands proves disastrous as the women are lacerated due to sexual exploitation.

The second group of lacerated women such as Aasha Rani (Starry Nights), Mikki (*Sisters*), Aparna and Rashmi (*Snapshots*) remain sincere in their marital relationship bearing all the atrocities of their husbands. But the husbands further humiliate the women through separation based on false accusations on their wives, While Karuna (*Socialite Evenings*) and Aparna (*Snapshots*) undergo the strain of legal separation through divorce. Aasha Rani (*Starry Nights*), Mikki (*Sisters*) and Rashmi (*Snapshots*) are forced to remain separated as they are chased out by the men. The women are shocked to find themselves suddenly anchorless and financially crippled in life. Confused and blinded to reason, the women opt of chaotic choices by getting entangled in extra marital relationships. Realising the futility of such relationship, the women continue to derive a kind of relief to their otherwise traumatized and agonized psyche.

Though the different childhood experiences undergone by the protagonists like Mikki and Alisha (*Sisters*), Nisha (*Sultry Days*), Noor (*Snapshots*), Asha Rani (*Starry Nights*). De stresses the ill-treatment meted out to girl children at the hands of the patriarchal parents that eventually denies them of self-respect and self-dignity. This leaves a feeling of insecurity in them. De delineates as to how her protagonists are made victims of dissipated marital relationships between the parents. As a result, De's protagonists in their childhood become victims of a loveless marital life. Obsessed with their own pleasures, the phallocentric fathers look down upon the girl children and dismiss them as trivial and trite. Apart from the autocratic, severe and stern attitude on the part of the fathers, there is absolutely not the slightest possibility for an emotional attachment or even communication between the girl children and their fathers. Gupta is therefore right when he asserts:

> It is needless to say that from her infancy, a female child lives in her parents attachment, and sees the world through their lives. So it is their father in whom she senses, first time, male domination and male ownership. She realizes how a man rules in every sphere from house to outside and how he refuses her value in every surrounding. She notices her mother to obey all commands of her husband. So a feeling of humiliation overcomes on her mind and heart for male hierarchy. (131)

Shobha De highlights a third variety of women, who themselves victims of male atrocities in one way or the other inflict similar atrocities on others. Their better experiences, combined with their aversion towards patriarchy and their obsession of a successful survival make them to be a kind of shrewish and selfish women. In their revolt against the male dominated society quite contradictorily they begin to resemble the male chauvinists in their attitudes towards others. Through the women Minx (*Strange Obsession*) and Aparna, Rashmi and Surekha (*Snapshots*) Shobha De shows how their victimization by the male chauvinists transforms them into hardhearted women who cease to feel for the suffering of others. Thus, Shobha De clearly shows how women in their frustration become blind to reason and their chaotic choices lead them towards emotional crisis. The bitter experiences undergone by Shobha De's women force them to realize the necessity to assert their individual self in a patriarchal society, the realization of their women self and their belief in the power of womanhood strength them mentally to overcome their victimized position. Shobha De's women prove assertive in their personal as well as professional lives. The women like Karuna, Anjali and Ritu (Socialite Evenings) tear off their cocoon of imagination and reconcile themselves with the traditional concept of marriage. In the modern age of technology and scientific advancements, man boasts of reaching the skies and touching the stars and planets. But when it comes to his domestic life, he experiences marital disharmony because of the male chauvinistic attitude ingrained in him. In the Indian male-dominated society, even before women enter into the marital phase, they are compulsorily made aware of the subdued status given to the wife in a marital relationship. In family life, the wife has no respectable role. She has no freedom to act but is always acted upon by men. Whatever may be the behavioural pattern of the husband, the wife is expected to show sublime reverence and follow his dictates without fail. Saxena asserts that:

> As individuals they may have progressed but in the institution of marriage the man is still the lord and master and a woman has to abide by his whims, and fancies whether she likes it or not. (261)

Shobha De herself, being hailed from a middle class family background, has great regard for the custom of marriage and she believes in the sanctity of marriage. Regarding marriage De opines:

> Marriage to me connotes commitment and surrender. Merging with, blending, overlapping, combining. It is a symbiotic relationship where one feeds on the other, depends on the other, needs the other. (*Selective Memory* 481)

Shobha De's career-women establish their assertiveness in their professional lives. The women are able to prove their mettle and individual powers in matters regarding business. They no longer remain passive and shadowy creatures, rather they possess the mental strength to outshine and astonish the male world surrounding them through their intellectual abilities. Shobha De's novels and on a note of reassurance, the women who had hostile and grim experiences emerge as individual beings with an identity of their own. As career-women, they assert their self and achieve economic independence. They succeed in freeing themselves from the bounded taboos of the social institutions like marriage and make progress through an assertive vision of life. Consequently, the new women are able to face life boldly overcoming all social barriers and restrictions. Shobha De's women characters trapped in a male dominated society are confronted with tiring situations that challenge the very existence of feminine individuality. The male-oriented society aims at crippling and demolishing the feminine- self by compulsively instilling the female sect with an internalized male world view. However, Shobha De's women with their inborn instinct towards establishing their individuality rebel against all acts of marginalization.

Shobha De in her novels concentrates on the serious issues such as the breakdown of morality in the modern urban society that is devoid of moral values. She critically analyses the unforeseen gaps and disruptions within the familial as well as societal framework which becomes the underlying reason for women's traumatized psyche. Though, host of critics have analysed the novels of Shobha De, and emphasized on the problems of women, no serious attempt is made so far in stressing on the continuous trauma suffered in the psychological as well as emotional level of her women. Her women undergo psycho-emotional trauma throughout their lives, because of the evil effects of gender discrimination. They have a haunting impact of insecurity. Therefore, the study is emphasized on how the Indian elite women confront the various suppressive attitudes that subjugate them for life and in the long process of struggle the women trun rebellions against tradition to escape the age old custom of male domination. The women characters of Shobha De emerge as New Women bent upon to assert the identity of womanhood in the present modern world. The novelist, who is known for her tremendous potential and vitality as a creative artist, thought her works succeed in exposing human life in its shallowness.

Shobha De is a social propagandist with a vision to bring about a cultural and moral reformation in the metropolitan life style. The underlying truth is that Shobha De as a novelist of repute, apart from her explicit narration of sexual matters is at the same time an author who can't be avoided or left unnoticed all that easily. She attributes to very serious themes such as gender discrimination, the impact of gender bias, female oppression, isolated childhood, lack of intimacy in child-paternal relationship, child sexual abuse and marital incompatibility. That is why Ramchandran rightly asserts when he comments: "One may love her or hate her but it is difficult to ignore her." (2:7)

Works Cited

Kamali. "Gender Discrimination and Feminist Awareness as depicted by Contemporary Tamil Writers", *Journal of Gender and Progress,* 1.1. Oct. 2003..

Prasad, Amar Nath. "A Brief History of Indian Women Novelists in English", *Indian Women Novelists in English.* New Delhi: Atlantic, 2001.

Paul, Samiran K. "Shobha De: A Postmodernist Woman Novelist Today", *The Indian Nation,* Patna, August 3, 1997.

Pushplata. "A Protest Among the Patriarchal in Shobha De's Works", *The fiction of Shobha De : Critical studies.,* Ed. Jaydipsinh Dodiya. New Delhi: Prestige, 2000.

Gupta, Rashmi. "Freedom from Social Bondage in Shobha De's *Sisters* and *Strange Obsession*", *Indian English fiction: Readings and Reflections.* Ed. Gajendra and Uday Shankar. New Delhi : Sarup and Sons, 2003.

Saxena, Alka. "Second Thoughts : A Slice of Urban Life", *The Fiction of Shobha De : Critical Studies, Ed.* Jaidipsinh Dodiya. New Delhi, Prestige, 2000.

De, Shobha. *Selective Memory : Stories from my Life.* New Delhi: Penguin, 1998.

Ramchandran, Janaki. "Survival Tactics", *The Hindu,* 02 Feb., 1997, Weekly ed.

13

Seeking the self: A Study of the Female Protagonists in Anita Nair's *Ladies' Coupe*

Kumkum Bhardwaj

Anita Nair is a name indelible in the arena of female Indian writers in English. Her books, set in the everyday world of India, mesmerize the reader with evocative language and descriptions. For Bangalore based author Anita Nair, Kerala is the source of inspiration, weakness and strength. In her works Nair presents the dilemmas that women face in their relationships with parents, husbands, siblings, friends, employers and children and their struggle towards self-realization. It is not easy to be a contemporary Indian woman. On the one hand she is aware of her rights and the need for an identity. On the other hand tradition dictates that she should submerge it in her role as daughter, sister, mother and wife. If a woman starts asserting her individuality then the transition from something else to her own identity is easy. But someone who subsumes herself into the identity of her husband and allows her other roles to contain her will find it difficult and wouldn't even know where to begin.

Nair's popular work *Ladies Coupe* (2001) is a tale of

the indomitable spirit of contemporary Indian women told with great insight and solidarity. In this novel she reflects the perpetual tension between the predicament of the contemporary Indian woman and the traditional Hindu culture. Nair's India suffers from a patriarchal system which has tried in many ways to repress, humiliate and debase women. The novel deals with multiple lives and multiple voices, where Nair answers a few questions that every woman would have faced in her life-questions related to her vulnerable position in society. The questions Nair poses in the novel, whether a single woman can really survive all by herself in this world or does she need a man to love her, protect her, and care for her? Nair has a humanitarian approach and is sensitive to Indian womanhood as being wronged. The answer that the novel provides is that 'there is a lot of strength in deep inside that every individual has' and that 'women must be courageous and claim their lives and possibilities.'

Nair's *Ladies Coupe* has been hailed as one of the most important feminist novels to come out of South India. However, there is none better than the novelist herself to talk about her own writing. In a chat with Suchitra Behal, Nair talks about her book: "I am not a feminist. I enjoy being in the house, I like to be treated nicely and pampered. I don't think this book is about feminism. It's about that inner strength which I see in so many women that overwhelms me. It doesn't come naturally. It has to be forced out of them; it could be circumstances or a change in lifestyle." Raising a question, "*Ladies Coupe* is a real life scenario in the lives of many Indian middle class women. How did you draw the inspiration for this novel?" She traces the origin of her book to 1998 when at the Bangalore station, "there was always a separate line for ladies, senior citizens and the handicapped....why they are being clubbed together, why women have to be treated like this. The book is about why women insist on using this line. When 15 years ago I was travelling in a ladies' coupe the women around me began talking — I was on the top berth – there is an atmosphere of intimacy that comes in. People talk more openly to strangers – there is no judgment." (Suchitra Behal)

At the onset, the story mainly concerns Akhilandeshwari, or Akhila- a forty five year old, unmarried, yearning to be independent, but has never been allowed to live her own life. A deep analysis of the novel reveals that the writer narrates stories of six women who are from different demographic and social backgrounds. The ladies coupe of a train bound to Kanyakumari finds these women thrown in proximity. They have nothing in common save their gender: some made happy marriages; some were not happy; one was raped and took her revenge, another seduced men much younger than herself. As strangers who know that they are never going to see each other again, and who have nothing to lose by baring their souls out, they tell each other about their lives. Once locked in together all six share their life stories, quite like the pilgrims do in Chaucer's Canterbury Tales and discover that they have never been living for themselves, but for others, governed by societal pressures. In a sense each story is separate but "their being together in one compartment provides the framework and holds the story together like a ribbon holding a bouquet of different kinds of flowers of different shapes, colours and fragrances." (Singh) Somewhere towards the end each story illuminates the story of Akhila who listens to all other women and tries to apply their views and justifications in comparison to her own life.

As women give more importance to relationships and affiliations, they always give priority to the needs and demands of others and sacrifice their own needs and desires for the sake of their home, merging their own identity in the process. In *Ladies Coupe,* Akhila is governed by societal pressures and does not live for herself, but for her family and the society, though it means sacrificing her own individual interests. She hails from a humble Tamil Brahmin family. Her father, a government servant, is the only breadwinner of the family, and who has to support his wife and four children. He is a very simple man far away from the office politics. Her mother is a typical traditional woman for whom her husband is no less than God. Since her childhood, Akhila has noticed that her parents are very much happy in each other's company. She could notice that they were able to communicate even without words. Sarsa Mani and Subramanian Iyer are their neighbours. Their family is also a happy family. Akhila has observed them so many times walking together and embracing each other.

As she is the eldest daughter in the family, after the death of her father Akhila accepts the entire responsibility and assumes the role of the head of the family. She starts working in an income tax office and toils hard for her family. Both her brothers and sister continue their studies and get good positions in life. They also married at the age they are supposed to. Akhila continues to look after her mother, siblings and their offspring who shamelessly keep sponging off her. No one seems to understand the fact that Akhila too needs to have a life of her own, married with children. Her mother seems to have accepted the idea that Akhila is a 'man', the head of the family, who has replaced her husband, Akhila's father. Gradually, in her daily quest to earn a living, Akhila loses her identity as a woman and starts living as a daughter, sister, colleaugue and an aunt later on.

It is at this juncture that Akhila searches for her identity. She wants to be Akhilandeshwari. She ponders about her life and what it has in store for her. Many times she has asked herself, "Who was Akhilandeshwari? Did she exist at all? If she did what was her identity?" (84) Akhila often thinks of a Tamil film 'Aval Oru Thodarkathai' she has seen some years ago, of a woman like her who dedicated her life for the love of her family. Akhila's firm conviction is that her family is to be blamed for her unmarried status. Akhila is ordinary in every sense of the word who has been brought up to become a good housewife and a good mother. So her longing for a happy married life is quite natural. Ultimately Akhila finds it in her relationship with Hari, a North Indian man, much younger to her.

The fear of society is a great impediment to personal freedom whether it is for a man or a woman. In a country that has always considered woman to be inferior being, it is the traditional norms that keep her tied down and the fear that if she were to swerve from the accepted path, she will be ostracized. Akhila and Hari both do take their time together and enjoy the time that they had alone. Akhila would have enjoyed security in this relationship but somehow, she thinks she has committed a sin by letting a boy as old as her younger brother enters her emotional and physical state. This fact constantly disturbs her, though Hari proclaims his deep love for her. She is disturbed when people stare at both of them wandering together and pass indecent comments. Besides, her sense of responsibility towards her family compels her to end the relationship though Hari is unwilling to. She maintains a distance from her love and decides to remain single. After this episode her life continues as usual. Nair beautifully sums up her protagonist, Akhila: "So this is Akhila. Forty five years old. Sans-rose coloured spectacles. Sans husband, children, home and family. Dreaming of escape and space. Hungry for life and experience. Aching to connect." (2) After Akhila's mother's death, the other members of the family, especially her brothers, discuss and decide where and with whom she should live. They decide it for her just because they are male members of the family. Akhila is taken for granted displaying a typical patriarchal attitude. Finally it is decided that she should live with her younger sister Padma's family. It is really ironic that an economically independent woman who took over the responsibility of the entire family years ago is not considered capable of looking after herself even at the age of forty five.

Akhila, living with Padma's family, continues to

tolerate the invasion of her privacy. Although Akhila supports Padma's family but Padma taking it for granted that Akhila would always need them does not miss a chance to criticize Akhila in every possible way. In fact Padma's marital status has empowered her to criticize her spinster sister. Padma as a typical representative shows how much value is attached to marriage in the Indian society. Her world not only revolves around cooking, cleaning, and taking care of the children, but also involves an adequate dose of how unfair and selfish working women were to their family and beyond. One day Akhila meets her school friend, Karpagam after a long gap. It is Karpagam who is able to instill a sense of self-worth in Akhila and makes her realize that she has every right to find happiness for herself. She makes Akhila realize to live her life on her own terms and not to be dictated by other members of her family who are actually dependent on her. Akhila, being fed up with Padma's behaviour decides to live alone in a single-bedroom apartment. It's a shock for the family that staunchly believes that a woman can never survive in the world all by herself, and naturally, they don't want her to go. Can a woman live alone? What will the society say? Ask brothers before taking a decision is the advice given by Padma. This reaction of Padma reveals the attitude of the society towards a single woman. But this time Akhila firmly declares that she has already fulfilled her duties towards her family, and now it is time for her to be alone. After a lot of pleading, Akhila finally agrees to think things over on a weekend trip all by herself for the first time in her life. So for the first time in her life, Akhila tries to get rid of all that her conservative Tamil Brahmin life has bound her in and plans to go by train somewhere she has never been before. Finally, without telling anyone, she boards the train to Kanyakumari to be by herself to discover herself.

Initially panic grips Akhila because she has never before been alone by herself. Various apprehensions and unanswered questions torment her by a nameless fear:

"How can I who have never spent a week away from my family survive a future alone? What do I know of running a household?....What do I know of life? How am I going to cope?" (21) Waiting for her train to come Akhila sees "Reunions. Farewells. A smile. Tears. Angers. Irritation. Anxiety. Boredom. Stillness" (2) - very much a part of her life too. As her journey progresses, Akhila finds herself crammed in a three-tiered women's compartment of a train travelling from Bangalore to Kanyakumari. Her fellow travellers, all females, are both curious and giving and sharing not only their tiffins but also their lives with her. After her initial resistance, Akhila strikes up a conversation with these women. In the intimacy of the female carriage she asks each of her travelling companions whether or not they think that a woman can be happy as a single woman living on her own. In this way she wants to convince herself that a woman can live alone. She "knew she could tell these women whatever she chose to. Her secrets, desires and fears. In turn, she could ask them whatever she wanted. They would never see each other again." (20) "Akhila thought they had established a connection. Fetuses jostling within the walls of a womb, drawing sustenance from each other's lives aided by the darkness outside and the fact that what was shared within the walls wouldn't go beyond this night or the contained space." (22)

Over the course of the journey each woman, ranging in age from 58 to 14, tells the story of her life in answer to Akhila's question. Two pampered matrons, a triumphantly angry teenager, a vengeful wife, and a mysterious woman share the most private moments of their lives. They talk about the men they loved, the men they hurt, the ones that they grew to be dependent on, and the ones they started to loathe. With strong portrayal of each character, Nair analyses the anguish and exuberance of her female protagonists. Between their tales Akhila reflects on her life and what little she has to show for it and her burgeoning desire to determine her own destiny.

Janaki Prabhakar, the oldest of the women, has been

married forty years, and like many marriages, hers has grown into a close, happy bond. In India a woman's sphere is restricted to her familial roles. Janaki is the example of a typical Hindu woman, pampered daughter, pampered wife who dares not raise a voice against any action of her husband. She believes that marriage is the male's authority over the female. Her husband has supported her all through her life and she does not know what to do in critical situations in life and thinks all is well with her life. She accepts, "I am a woman who has always been looked after. First there was my father and my brothers, then my husband. When my husband is gone, there will my son. Women like me end up being fragile. Our men treat us like princesses. And because of that we look down upon women who are strong and who can cope with themselves." (22-23) Janaki has no hesitation in accepting the fact that in accommodation lay her true happiness. She apprehends painfully that there is nothing to do with emotions for old people. There is a perfect combination between them. She frankly tells her husband that 'I am tired of sharing you with everyone, I want you to myself.' A short stay at their son's house makes her realize that she has developed 'friendly love for her husband at this stage of life.' Janaki also talks of her sudden disinterest in that same home, of her sudden urge to be a confident being, no longer fragile. But at the end she says that even if she were alone and even though she managed to cope alone "it would be the same if he wasn't there with me." (pg. 23) Janaki's story disturbes her a lot and Akhila is left wondering if she had made a mistake by wishing to escape, escape from loneliness.

Prabha Devi, a rich woman finds her life empty and does not go by the norms set by society. She is a woman who is completely assured of who she is and likes to be the way she is on. However, she understands and appreciates the sanctity of marriage. Initially Prabha Devi is happy with her fate. When she accompanies her husband to New York, she gets fascinated with the western culture where a woman is as liberated as a man. "Their lives were ruled by themselves and no one else. Such power, such confidence, and celebration of life and beauty." (177) This trip changes her. Prabha Devi becomes conscious of her beauty and sexuality. She starts reading magazines and visits beauty parlours very often. After coming to India she lives her life like a westernized woman. She looks more charming, beautiful, sensuous and confident woman. The change in her is remarkable and it gives her immense satisfaction. But when she tries to lure Pramod by her beauty as one day he comes home thinking her to be 'like these women' Prabha Devi is shocked. She immediately comes out of her dream world and realizes her mistake. Once again she enters into her own cocoon and becomes 'grahini'. She engages herself in performing the role of an ideal wife and an obedient daughter-in-law. For many years she enjoys the security of married life. As Prabha Devi has her own opinions and plans for her life, many years later she plans to learn swimming that too without her husband's knowledge. The glimpse of a swimming pool made her decide that she would learn how to swim. And she does! For her learning to swim, which she does without anybody's help is actually a means to establish her individuality, a way of discovering her existence. In this process she triumphs over her innate timidity and rediscovers her old carefree self who does not bother of what people will say. Her whole life is transformed as "She felt the years slip away from her...from the tips of her fingers, a straight line a slow triumph...my body no longer matters. I have this. I have conquered fear." (195) Akhila thinks if Prabha Devi could triumph over her innate timidity and rise above traditions to float, she can do the same. She too must learn to move on with the tide of life rather than be precipitated on its bank.

Sheela Vasudevan, a fourteen year old girl is endowed with an ability to perceive what others cannot. At this tender age, she understands many things. She does not like her father's way of approaching towards problems.

She is much influenced by her grandmother Ammumma who was an ardent worshipper of beauty and who hated imperfections of any kind. Sheela is imaginative enough to understand her granny that she defies and loathes the obscenities of death and age. When her grandmother dies of cancer and her body was prepared for funeral, young Sheela remembers her granny's lesson to her, "The only person you need to please is yourself." (67) Sheela dresses up her dead grandmother's body in costume, jwellery and make up because she cannot bear to have her face the world looking so unprepared. Sheela's story provides a new direction to Akhila. Instead of bothering about others, she should please her own self.

Margaret Paulraj, a chemistry lecturer, is married to the person of her choice still their marriage does not work. Her husband, Ebenezer Paulraj, Principal of a public school in Coimbatore inflicts great emotional violence on her. She is seen by her husband as an object to fulfill his desires. He successfully destroys Margaret's self-confidence by bullying her and shouldering all the responsibilities of the household. She wants to do Ph.D. but he suggests that she should go for in B.Ed. When she conceives he convinces her to undergo an abortion. When she expresses her doubt if the Church would approve the act, he argues: "first of all, the Bible never mentions the word abortion....If you had a boil that turned septic wouldn't you have it lanced? Just think of this as a tumour that has to be removed." (106) Her family members are unable to believe that she is unhappy. His artificial politeness, warmth, cruelty, constant contempt of Margaret, his favourite theories and his habit of defacing books by ugly drawings are facets of his personality hidden from the world. Margaret tolerates all the contempt from the 'most loved' husband but remains silent. There seems to be no way out, until one day she discovers a gold fish floating dead. This proves to be a turning point of her life. She decides to be evasive to him in order to touch and shake his self-esteem, the very foundation of his being. In her own way, she avenges herself by over feeding him and making him so dependent on her that he would need her in every step he takes. There is complete reversal of role. Earlier Ebe used to control her life, now she has him completely in her hands. "Ebe slowly became a fat man. A quiet man. An easy man. A man who no longer needed the Coterie or defaced books... he needed me like he had never before. And Ebe became a man I could live with once again." (134)

It is more credible as she does so without breaking family or making parents unhappy by seeking divorce. Margaret knows the society well. When her marriage did not work, people thought they were doing well, and when Margaret mended things her way, it went even smoother. Margaret feels proud to narrate her life story. How she tames her husband and how she succeeds and attains peace after spoiling her husband's pride over his athletic figure. She does not compel Akhila to follow her views but the one thing she tells Akhila becomes the crux of the novel: "You'll discover that once you stop worrying what the world will think of you, your life will become that much easier to live. Just remember that you have to look out for yourself. No one else will." (136)

Marikolanthu or Mary, thirty one year old single parent who feels sorry for the silk worm, she who talks to worms, trees and rocks in her childhood speaks about her journey from an innocent girl to a woman. She has been a rape victim and has a son by that union. Now she is a woman "from whom anger paused forth like a stream of lava." (209) A single woman has no significance in our society. Mary is a glaring example of a woman's plight who has seen love, hate, pain, anger, and compassion from both sides of the coin in her life. She tells, "I was a restless spirit raped and bitter, sometimes I would think of the past and I would feel a quickening in the vacuum that existed within me now." (266) After the rape, unsurprisingly, it is Mary who is to be blamed-why does a young woman walk alone?

Marikolanthu's views and philosophy of life are

different from other fellow passengers. She believes in the destiny written by Brahma. According to her Brahma allots a specific number of years to each one to experience all aspects of life. She learns great lesson from the most trifling moments in life and thereby moulds her own philosophy. Mary is angry about the fuss the other travellers made about what she thought were little things. She wonders what they would do if real tragedy confronted them. She believes they couldn't comprehend how cruel the world could be to women. Hers is the most horrifying story of a woman raped, caste out, abandoned, extremely poor, beyond hope, a thirty one year old woman with a son and no husband. "Women", she said however, "are strong. Women can do everything as well as men. Women can do much more. But a woman has to seek that vein of strength in herself. It does not show itself naturally." (210)

Thus each chapter of the novel is devoted to one of the women's stories depicting their personal crisis such as loneliness, ill treatment, rape, abortion, madness, betrayal and how each one coped with them. Each woman has gone through some kind of struggle as each of them tells her about the moments they were the happiest and the moments they wished never happened. Janaki, Prabha Devi and Margaret and Akhila are victims of 'Pygmalion effect'. They are examples of adjustments. Janaki and Prabha Devi do not feel complete without a man. Deep in their hearts, they think, world has no use for a single woman. Janaki realizes that she has no identity as such, she is very traditional. However, Prabha Devi tries to obtain sexual autonomy without understanding its complications. She tries to flout the tradition by secretly learning how to swim. Margaret is educated, financially independent but even then has become crippled. She believes that a woman needs a man but not to make her complete. Though economically independent in life, Akhila herself follows the tradition and waits for her family to choose spouse for her and is afraid of the society. She is bothered about her lovers' age and what people will say if she marries him against the norm. Akhila realizes that all these women are tied to the bonds of the family life and in turn want the security of married life. They are traditional in the sense that they have drawn a borderline for themselves and they do not have the courage to cross it.

Nair uses a special technique that weaves the past, present and future of Akhila in the story. She recollects her past, listens to others and moulds her future. In this way she goes through the experience of all the ladies in the coupe. Travelling in the train and lulled asleep Akhila slips occasionally into a past. Nair tenderly draws Akhila's family scenes and builds up her story into something very absorbing. Her two brothers found job, they decided to get married not once asking, "What about you? You've been the head of this family ever since Appa died. Don't you want a husband, children, a home of your own?" (77) Her younger sister had to get married as the 'little one' had changed into 'a woman'-Ammma had told her. Akhila, at thirty four, single and lonely. Her single form of revolt is seen when she wants to taste a boiled egg brought by her Anglo Indian colleague, Katherine Webber who teaches her how to eat an egg. "My mother always says that eating an egg without salt is like kissing a man without moustache." (88) She dreams of a lustful encounter with a stranger. The dream ends with her family calling her 'shameless creature' and 'a brazen slut'. She awakes startled and ashamed of her behaviour.

However, one of the marked features of the book is the absence of Akhila's own identity. Is this a sad reality of today's woman? That she is unable to carve out an identity for herself? Akhila is not an exceptionally strong woman. She is full of desires. All she wanted was to be a good wife and mother- the simple dream of a simple woman. But she is not given the opportunity by her family to get married and have a family, as traditions dictate. After hearing out these five women and their stories of living in a cocoon sheltered by men or rampant exploitation again by men, Akhila realizes that there is so much more to life than the confines of her small bank cubicle, her grumpy family, and her lonely self. She understands that what needs to be done, needs to be done now and suddenly decides to take her life in her hands. "Akhila is certain that she won't let her family use her anymore....For within me is a woman I have discovered." (270) All these women, Akhila muses, Janaki, Sheela, and even Margaret who wears her self-sufficiency as a halo, are trying to make some sense of their own existence by talking about it to anyone who will listen. I am the same, she thought. I'm trying to define the reality of my life, justify my failures and my own sense of hopelessness by preying on the fabric of their lives, seeking in it a similar thread that in some way will connect their lives with mine, make me feel less guilty for who I am and what I have let myself become. Indeed at the end, she feels she has her own life to live and becomes confident and empowered to reclaim her lost love.

Relationship of any sort calls for change. A woman has to change her attitude while performing her varied roles as wife, mother, daughter, or daughter-in-law. Discovery for existence here is more a guidance for assertion and realization of one's own interests, certainly not selfish in the narrow sense. When Akhila reaches Kanyakumari, she stays alone in a hotel and decides to make her own private rebellion. Perhaps her loneliness or her desire to feel happy and wanted again urges her to start a relationship with Vinod who is younger to her. It is, in fact, Akhila who initiates the relationship, which has no emotional involvement on the part of both. She feels as if she is released from the hold of convention and family expectations. Now she is mentally prepared to face the consequences of her decision. She is not bothered about what others would say. After Vinod's departure, she calls her old lover Hari and we understand that a man replies at the other end, who, probably, is Hari. Whether their relationship will continue or not is left to our imagination. But it is clear Akhila's quest for self-discovery is complete, her identity crisis has overcome. The idea of self-realization urges her to withdraw from her meaningless seclusion towards new awareness and initiates her union with Hari a better relationship.

In this novel Nair studies the social forces working on the psychology of the Indian woman. All the women, in one way or the other, present their own need for existence and independence. By narrating the stories of these six women, Nair moves them from a state of passivity and absence into a state of active presence, from the kitchen and the bedroom to the street and the world at large. These are the stories, which together make a single story, of women rediscovering their existence. However, this does not imply that these women today wish to disturb the existing social and economic parameters. They are aware of their exploitations, conscious of their rights and willingly though assertively compromise with situations. In such a world, all the female protagonists become bold enough to recognize the demand of their own self and ready to take responsibility of their lives.

Janaki's relationship with her husband is full of Friendly love, understanding, and loyalty. P rabha Devi loves swimming because it, metaphorically, gives her a sense of achievement. Margaret succeeds in 'disciplining' her narcissistic husband and manages to survive by sheer will power. Sheela's ability to perceive what others cannot paves the way for her own future liberation. Marikolanthu, whose innocence was destroyed by one night of lust, manages to survive by sheer will power. And finally, Akhila manages to replace fear by self-confidence which is an essential ingredient for happiness in the life of a woman. "What then is the purpose of life. What exactly are we looking for? The usual answer is happiness. 'Define happiness,' asks one of the women in the coupe. Akhila quotes words of a New Year's greeting card: "Happiness is being allowed to choose one's own life; to live it the way one wants. Happiness is knowing one is loved and having someone to love. Happiness is able to hope for tomorrow." (200)

Akhila's railway journey to Kanyakumari needs to be studied from another perspective also. Kanyakumari is a pilgrimage town at the very tip of India. It occupies a special place in Akhila's mind, since it "had got its name from the goddess who, like her, is unmarried and eternally waiting for her groom to arrive." (3) Finding herself adrift with no life of her own, she expects the answers to her questions to emerge from the sea at Kanyakumari. "Just as Vivekananda flung himself into the churning waters and the salts of the three seas and swam to a rock upon which he sat resolutely, waiting for answers that had eluded him all his life." (3) Besides, Nair deliberately uses the fictional strategy of the ladies compartment to bring her six characters together. The title refers to the carriage exclusively for elderly people, handicapped, and women, a practice in India which lasted until 1998. The word 'coupe' suggests confined or restricted or closed space. Akhila's world, indeed, has been a confined space. Akhila's railway journey to Kanyakumari also becomes a pilgrimage of sorts, as her companions in the all-women sleeping car - the ladies coupé - are mates not only in her physical journey but also in her spiritual and psychological journeys. Where else but in a train would strangers reveal and bare their innermost souls with such freedom and abandon? In this sense the coupe becomes a metaphor for a utopian world that is liberated from patriarchy, one that is not characterised by false binaries. Even though, as Anita Nair tells us in an author's note at the end of the book, the ladies queue and the ladies coupe are no more (presumably because the railways authorities have decided that women no longer need special concessions), women's stories, such as the ones we hear in this book.

Thus the novel provides a deep insight into the lives of women in modern-day India, illustrating their tough battle for an opening and the restrictions which are still exerted by tradition, religion and convention. After reading *Ladies Coupe,* one observes that Indian womanhood is changing. The life stories of these women give an insight into the expectations of married Indian women the choices they make, and the choices made for them. What is remarkable in the novel is that it conveys a strong message of hope through change. From typical Indian middle class traditional woman Akhila changes to a transitional woman. The character of Akhila is symbolic of all those who are in quest for self-realization. She wants fulfillment in life, first, gratification of sexual needs, and then, motherhood. Her experience conveys the message that a woman can survive and get her identity not by keeping herself isolated from male-dominated society, but by cooperating with them. A strong feeling emerges from the novel that women like Akhila want simple things from the society and that is, they should be considered and treated as human beings first and foremost not as women or sexual commodities.

Works Cited

Nair, Anita. *Ladies Coupe*. New Delhi: Penguin Books, 2001. (All references from this book are from this edition.)

Kalamani, N. *The Fusing Horizons: Critical Essays in Indian Writing*. New Delhi: Atlantic Publishers, 2008.

Clara, Nubile. *The danger of Gender: Caste, Class and Gender in Contemporary Indian Women's Writing*. New Delhi: Sarup & Sons, 2003.

Sree, S.P. *Psychodynamics of Women in the Post Modern Literature*. New Delhi: Sarup & Sons, 2006.

Sinha, Sunita. *Post Colonial Women Writers: New Perspectives*. New Delhi: Atlantic Publishers, 2008.

Menon, Bindu. *Ladies Coupe Was Harder to Write: An Interview with Anita Nair*, Caffedilli.com

Behal, Suchitra. *Writing for Oneself*. Caffedilli.com

Literary Review. The Hindu. http//hinduonet.com/thehindu/2001/12/02

Singh, Khushwant. *Article: travelling in a Women's Compartment*. Tribune. Saturday, March 22, 2002.

14

Kiran Desai's *The Inheritance of Loss*: An Estimate

M.S. Wankhede

Kiran Desai, as far as the field of novel is concerned, is a name that has popularity in the whole world nowadays. Her tragi-comic novel *The Inheritance of Loss* spans two continents and three generations, for which she has claimed Britain's most prestigious literary award, Man Booker Prize, in 2006 and has won the National Book Critics Circle Award in 2007 and Orange Prize for Fiction in the same year. The story of this novel cuts between New York and India, contrasting the menial jobs and meager conditions of immigrant life in the city with the political unrest engulfing an isolated Himalayan hill town. At 35, Desai was the youngest woman and second female fiction-writer after Arundhati Roy ever to win the Man Booker Prize. *The Inheritance of Loss* is her second novel. The judges hailed *The Inheritance of Loss* as "a magnificent novel of humane breadth and wisdom, comic tenderness and powerful political acuteness."

Today Indian writing in English has achieved the water table mark but the problem before Indian writers in English was quite different. The Indian writers were using an erstwhile colonial language to express their world-views and vision of social reality. Indian writing in English serves a great purpose, today. It has variety of literary genres. Particularly, Indian fiction in English has been enriched by several highly talented women novelists including Kamala Markandaya, Anita Desai, Nayantara Sahgal, Attia Hosain, Santha Rama Kau and Shashi Deshpande, etc. Kiran Desai, the daughter of Anita Desai, is also now one of the women novelists of international repute. Among the critics and historians of literature are K. R. Srinivas Iyengar, C. D. Narashimhaiah and M. K. Naik.

At present our Indian society is experiencing tremendous transformation, affecting its complexion and ideas. Especially last four to five decades brought about radical changes in every walk of life. The novel, in the Indian context, is the product of the second part of the nineteenth century. K. R. Srinivasa Iyengar observes:

> The 'novel' as a literary phenomenon is new to India. Epics, lyrics, dramas, short stories and fables have their respectable ancestries, going back by several centuries, but it is only during a period of little more than a century that the novel- the long sustained piece of prose fiction- has occurred and taken root in India. ... Novels have been, and are being published in a dozen Indian languages, and also in English; and the reciprocal influence between the novel in English and novel in the regional languages has been rather more intimate and purposive than such influence in the fields of poetry or drama. (Iyenger 314)

Literature, which is essentially a social and cultural seismograph, records the throbbing pulse of time and transmutes it into the heartbeat of eternity. The independent India has witnessed a creative upsurge of ideas of arts and literature. Pre and post-independent India provided a number of subjects for the Indian writers in English to write about with different attitudes. In 1947, when India got independence, Indians faced sensitive problems on the socio-political and cultural fronts as well. The partition of India had left in its wake the breathtaking task of restoring peace and confidence among the people who were ragged by the lethal outbursts of communal fury, political disharmony, massive social disparities, civic corruption, and lack of meaningful cohesive forces in society. In a multilingual country like India, creative writers began to record the social truths and emotional verities in their respective languages. Indian English novelists have been showing deep concern about these problems also. Thus they began to write on variety of topics in the post-independent India.

Kiran Desai has written her second novel in lyrical prose which explores such themes as colonialism, illegal migration and political strife. She has written the novel of depth and complexity. She has filled it with multiple characters and beautiful prose that is lyrical in nature. While writing this novel Desai perhaps ignored certain Indian things. In an interview she expresses: "I will admit to being somewhat overwhelmed at times due to my immigration and Indian history, class and politics. In fact, this book forced me to do something I seldom do - research the history and geography of the area. What I discovered is a country which is vast in its scope and complicated in its history." (www.caribousmom.com) *The Inheritance of Loss* has the issues of colonialism and globalization as constant themes. It speaks to Kiran Desai's gift as a writer that she tackles these immense issues with ease using eloquent prose. She artfully weaves together the stories of several characters, moving from the present day (1980's) to their past histories without a malfunction. She examines life in the town Kalimpong in India and New York City. The struggle for cultural identity is a common theme of the novel.

The Inheritance of Loss takes up a number of subjects such as morality and justice, globalization, racial, social and economic inequality, fundamentalism and alienation.

It takes its reader on a see-saw of negative emotions. In short, in the digression of the sub-plots, the novel is a unique one. The book is a link of the East with the West. There is a conflict in India, a country in the Asian Continent, representing the East, and the East has a clash with the West, in a variety of things The main story is about the kinds of losses the characters endure. Kiran Desai is a clinical expositor of culture and human nature rather human nature more than a mere narrator of lives that draw the reader in. *The Inheritance of Loss* is, as the name suggests, a story of loss as well as power struggles. While some pay the price for their circumstances emotionally, others lose material things. The plot is set against the backdrop of ethnic strife in northern India. However, this is not the only struggle that shapes the plot. A picture of the economic disparity and its effects on society is also cleverly depicted in the novel. With a keen eye for telling detail and profound wisdom, Kiran Desai weaves the webs of colonial history with its slow burn of humiliation, and creates a rich tapestry of characters that live with questions of identity and alienation, exiles at home and abroad.

The woman of today is a mother, wife and daughter and amidst all she struggles to keep her own identity. After getting into close study of Kiran Desai, it comes to knowledge that she has created her own identity as a woman writer. Woman in Kiran Desai, it seems, deconstructs literary forms and socio-political constructs. In the process, the writer has shown a remarkable extension of her vision, a maturity as an artist ready to venture into new areas of narrative art. She has adopted new techniques in order to sound those depths of psychology that perhaps only a few dared before. Kiran Desai's novel is also a tale of the effects of globalization on individuals and on communities while efficiently illustrating the indissoluble bonds of love and family. It is indeed a love story involving a boy (Gyan) and a girl (Sai), a father (the cook of the retired judge, Jemulal) and son (Biju), and also a grandfather (the judge) and his grand-daughter (Sai), where empathy and compassion often define the quality of family relationship. Kiran Desai manages the combination of the East and the West. Hence she responds to her interviewer:

> Being part of the Indian Diaspora gives one a precise emotional location to work from, if not a precise geographical one. This book was a return journey to the fact of being Indian, to realizing the perspective was too important to give up. America might give me half a narrative, but I had to return to India for the other half of the story, for emotional depth, historical depth. I don't care about passports. Literature is located beyond flags and anthems, simple ideas of loyalty. The vocabulary of immigration, of exile, of translation, inevitably overlaps with a realization of the multiple options for reinvention, of myriad perspectives, shifting truths, telling of lies— the great big wobbliness of it all. In a world obsessed with national boundaries and belonging, as a novelist working with a form also traditionally obsessed with place, it was a journey to come to this thought, that the less structured, the multiple, may be a possible location for fiction, perhaps a more valid ethical location in general. (www.guardian.co.uk)

The Inheritance of Loss opens with a teenage Indian girl, an orphan named Sai, living with her Cambridge-educated Anglophile grandfather, a retired judge in the town Kalimpong in the Himalayas. Sai is romantically involved with her mathematics tutor Gyan, the successor of a Nepali Gurkha mercenary. But he eventually withdraws from her apparent privilege and falls in with a group of ethnic Nepalese rebel. In the other parallel narrative, we are shown the life of Biju, the son, a cook working with Sai's grandfather. Biju belongs to the "shadow class" of illegal immigrants in New York and spends much of his time evading the authorities. He moves from one ill-paid job to another. But what makes these apparently disparate characters come together is a shared historical heritage and a common experience of powerlessness and humiliation. Referring to centuries of subjection by the economic and cultural power of the West, Desai remarks 'Certain moves made long ago had produced all of them' but the beginning of an apparently levelled field in a late-20th century global economy serves merely to scratch those wounds rather than heal them.

The novel centres on a retired judge, his grand-daughter, Sai, the cook, the cook's son Biju, and Gyan, the tutor of Sai. All these characters are flawed and try to seek fulfilment. They all experience loss as the story unstitches. All through the novel the Judge is an unhappy man. He has little love in his heart for anyone except Mutt, his dog. And he is filled with hatred for all other Indians. He wishes he had been born English. This is an inheritance of loss. Biju, the son of cook, also experiences this ambivalence for Indian people. He experiences rejection and racism as an illegal immigrant living in America: "The habit of hate had accompanied Biju and he found that he possessed an awe of white people who arguably had done India great harm, and a lack of generosity regarding almost everyone, who had never done a single harmful thing to India." (86) The three of them- the cook, the judge and the young teen-age girl- are helpless, unwilling witnesses to the identity struggle playing out in the hills as the GNLF and other parties claim a land, a language and a respect that have all already been denied the Nepali immigrants turned settlers. The characters in *The Inheritance of Loss* are insecure and unmoored, and are frequently struggling to survive in the modern world. They are unsure of whether they will ever see the benefits and profits of globalization. Kiran Desai doesn't present any easy answers to the problems of those who are left behind by unstoppable economic growth.

Like some of her characters, Desai has a foot in two countries. Brought up in India, England, and the United

States, she now divides her time between Brooklyn and New Delhi. But the influence on her writing is more one-sided. As she told *The Guardian* after winning the Man Booker Prize, "I realize that I see everything through the lens of being Indian." The focus of the novel is on the fate of a few powerless individuals, but Kiran Desai manages to explore, with intimacy and insight, every contemporary international issue: globalization, multiculturalism, economic inequality, fundamentalism and terrorist violence. Despite being set in the mid -1980's, it seems the best kind of post-9/11 novel. Desai takes a skeptical view of the West's consumer-driven multiculturalism, noting the "sanitized elegance" of Lola's daughter's British-accented voice, which is "triumphant over any horrors the world might thrust upon others." At such moments, Desai seems far from writers like Zadie Smith and Hari Kunzru, whose fiction takes a generally optimistic view of what Salman Rushdie has called "hybridity, impurity, intermingling, the transformation that comes of new and unexpected combinations of human beings, cultures, ideas, politics, movies, songs." In fact, Desai's novel seems to argue that such multiculturalism, confined to the Western metropolis and academic, doesn't begin to address the causes of extremism and violence in the modern world.

Almost all of Desai's characters have been stunted by their encounters with the West. As a student, isolated in racist England, the future judge feels "barely human at all" and leaps "when touched on the arm as if from an unbearable intimacy." But on his return to India, he finds himself despising his apparently backward Indian wife. Thus it seems that the judge is one of those "ridiculous Indians," as the novel puts it, "who couldn't rid themselves of what they had broken their souls to learn" and whose Anglophilia can only turn into self-hatred. These Indians are also an unwanted anachronism in postcolonial India. Here long-suppressed peoples have begun to awaken to their dereliction and to express their anger and despair.

For some of Desai's characters, including one of the judge's neighbours in Kalimpong, this comes as a distinct shock: "Just when Lola had thought it would continue, a hundred years like the one past – Trollope, BBC, a burst of hilarity at Christmas – all of a sudden, all that they had claimed innocent, fun, funny, not really to matter, was proven wrong." For those readers with extensive knowledge about this region, *The Inheritance of Loss* will reverberate. But for those readers who do not have the base of that knowledge, the novel will lose some of its power. Even then the novel remains equally readable for all.

The clash of civilizations is persistent in the novel "The Loss of Inheritance." The novel may strike many readers as offering an unrelentingly bitter view, though much humour has been alive there in it. Set in India in a small Himalayan community along the border with Nepal, its centre is the once grand, now decaying home of a melancholy retired judge, his valiant cook, and beloved dog, Sai, the judge's teenage granddaughter, has just moved in, and she finds herself trapped in a shadowy fairy tale-like life in a majestic landscape where nature is so rambunctious that it threatens to overwhelm every human quest for order. Just as Kiran Desai has hesitated in accepting American citizenship, she has been unwilling to embrace the American style of writing.

Sitting on the verandah Sai was reading an article about giant squid in an old National Geographic. "Every bow and then she looked up at Kanchenjunga, observed its wizard phosphorescence with a shiver." (2) Soon she closed the magazine and walked into the garden: "The forest was old and thick at the edge of the lawn; the bamboo thickets rose thirty feet into the gloom; the trees were moss-slung giants, bunioned and misshapen, tentacled with the roots of orchids. The caress of the mist through her hair seemed human, and when she held her fingers out, the vapour took them gently into its mouth." (6) The clash in the eastern continent is quiet clear from the threatening by the young boys of GNLF (Gorkha National Liberation Front):

> "Say, 'Jai Gorkha," they said to the judge. "Gorkhaland for Gorkhas."
> "Jai Gorkhas."
> "Say. 'I am a fool.'"
> "I am a fool."
> "Loudly. Can't hear you, *huzoor*. Say it louder."
> He said it in the same empty voice.
> "Jai Gorkha," said the cook, and "Gorkhaland for Gorkhas," said Sai,
> although they had not been asked to say anything.
> "I am a fool," said the cook. (2)

Biju's father (the cook with the retired judge) has sent his only son to America. He did so because he wanted his son seek better life. The cook of the retired judge hopes for contentment and dignity and he believes that it will come with his son's success:

> He imagined sofa, TV, bank account. Eventually Biju would make enough and the cook would retire. He would receive a daughter-in-law to serve him food, crick-crack his toes, grandchildren so swat like flies. Time might have died in the house that on the mountain ledge, its grown indistinct with moss, its roof loaded with ferns, but with each letter, the cook trundled toward future. (17)

After losing her parents, Sai, the granddaughter of the retired judge, comes to live with her grand father and imagines a life of love: "Could fulfillment ever be felt as deeply as loss? Romantically she decided that love must surely reside in the gap between desire and fulfilment, in the lack, not the contentment. Love was the ache, the anticipation, the retreat, everything around it but the emotion itself." (2-3) Like many important works of literature, the book can be read on several levels— as an inventive, fast-moving, delicious tale, which is full of rich descriptions and marvellous comic cartoon-like personalities, but also as a deeper study of the pathos of familial misunderstanding, the absurdity of hero-worship, the impulsiveness of commercialism and the clumsiness of bureaucracy.

Gyan, the Mathematics tutor of Sai, is born of poverty and proudly Indian. His family's house is still made of mud with a thatch roof. He feels demoralized by the judge's very English and superior ways. He is also fed up with the fact that Indian-Nepalese are being treated like the minority in a place where they are the majority. In their native land they have been treated badly by the settlers. As a result he rejects Sai's privileged life. Intent to scream victory over oppression, Gyan raised his fist to authority, eventually connecting with a crowd of angry Nepalese insurrectionists. On the other hand young Biju, the judge's cook's son, ekes out an existence as an undocumented worker in New York City. Stumbling from one low-paid restaurant job to another, Biju lives with groups of other immigrant men. He imagines what life would be like with "a sofa, TV and a bank account." The cook believes in the success of his son.

But Biju came to the States thinking that he could achieve the American dream, but the reality is quite different. It's "a whole world of basement kitchens," living so intensely with others only to have them disappear overnight, one giant "shadow class" of men. The novel describes the resolution of the cultural clash- the clash between the East and the West as well as a clash within the East too. The cultural clash matters a lot, which can be understood from the answer given by the author herself to one of her interviewers: "It's the rhythm of a writing life that comes from 50 years of working, and from that older time of being a writer in India when you wrote for writing's sake alone, not for the cocktail *samosas*." (www.Amazon.com) These words can be a result from a writer only when she is quite aware of the cultures which she narrates in her book. Alternating between Biju's struggle to survive in the New York City and the steadily gathering insurgency of men and guns in the hills of

Kalimpong, Kiran Desai portrays a world on the cusp of globalization, desperately trying to cope with a rapid modernization. Kiran Desai's characters are stubborn and arrogant, often refusing to cast off the structures of colonialism yet continuing to struggle with loss, poverty, and the trappings of their social class. Thus the characters are cultural conscious. It could be quite worthy to mention especially the two characters- Biju and his father, the cook with the retired Civil Service judge, the English-educated Indian, who has started living in a small town called Kalimpong, in the Himalayas.

Published to extraordinary acclaim, *The Inheritance of Loss* heralds Kiran Desai as one of our most insightful novelists. She illuminates the pain of exile and the ambiguities of post-colonialism with a tapestry of colorful characters: an embittered old judge; Sai, his sixteen-year-old orphaned granddaughter; a chatty cook; and the cook's son, Biju, who is hop-scotching from one miserable New York restaurant to another, trying to stay a step ahead of the INS. When a Nepalese insurgency in the mountains threatens Sai's new-sprung romance with her handsome tutor, their lives descend into chaos. The cook witnesses India's hierarchy being overturned and discarded. The judge revisits his past and his role in Sai and Biju's intertwining lives. A story of depth and emotion, hilarity and imagination, *The Inheritance of Loss* tells a story of love, family, and loss. Kiran Desai has taken a great task to write such novel as *The Inheritance of Loss.*

Hermione Lee, chairwoman of the judges, said: "I think her mother would be proud. It is clear to those of us who have read Anita Desai that Kiran Desai has learned from her mother's work. Both write not just about India but about Indian communities in the world. The remarkable thing about Kiran Desai is that she is aware of her Anglo-Indian inheritance - of Naipaul and Narayan and Rushdie - but she does something pioneering. She seems to jump on from those traditions and create something which is absolutely of its own. The book is movingly strong in its humanity and I think that in the end is why it won." Although Kiran Desai has been praised by many of her fans, she has been bitterly criticized.

Ashok Mantravadi observes: "What a miserable book this is.... The only reason I finished it was that I had nothing else with me on a recent flight. ... That this is a worthless piece of fiction is easy to conclude – the characters are all hollow, one dimensional and uninteresting; the two parallel narratives do not get anywhere and do not combine in any interesting way; at no point is there any kind of dramatic tension; and the writing style is pretentious. What is more bothersome is the enormous negativity in the book...." (Amazon) In the same manner M. Galishoff states: "I was disappointed by all of the hype and rave reviews this book was given. The author has good subject matter but has chosen a most difficult and almost incoherent writing style in which to convey her thoughts. The novel jumps from place to place faster than rabbit being chased by a fox. ... The prose is choppy, awkward and at times obscured by so much symbolism as to be obscure and unintelligible." (Amazon) Japan reader says: "This book is grossly over-rated. I've tried to read it twice but finally abandoned the effort." (Ibid) Similarly Hindol Datta U.S.A. expresses: "I am surprised that Ms. Desai won the Bookers for this book. It is very poorly written with a lot of clichés and panders to the stereotypes of the Western readers." (Amazon)

One of the admirers of the book says that Kiran Desai has written an exquisite novel which deserves the Booker Award and its place on the New York Times Most Notable Fiction list. This is a novel to be savoured for its stunning prose, complex characters and finely captured sense of place. Kiran Desai reveals the rigid adherence to the class system in simple ways. She also uncovers the pain of being an illegal immigrant. On a positive note Kiran Desai is mistress of details. The story has been set against a background of a beautiful town at the foot of the Himalayas. The author asserts Indian values- or lacks thereof- in her characters denoting her readers with Indian's lifestyle and tradition. The book has a lot of history anecdotes which have been painstakingly researched by the novelist. She captures her reader's attention with multiculturalism and her definition of the different forms of love, giving an edge to the book compared to other fictions in the market. There is no denying the book is beautifully written. Every word has been cleverly chosen giving the text an overall thoughtful and thorough description. *The Inheritance of Loss* offers all of the pleasures of traditional narrative in a form and a voice that are utterly fresh. It is at once a novel of class and economic disparity on post-colonial India with its fading anglophiles, their crumbling edifices and their dwindling power in the face of a modernizing nation's disaffected population. Kiran Desai's language, both vivid and wicked, her keen sense of detail and her fine ear for dialogue keep the whole story from just sliding downhill. Her greatest virtue lies in her being able to infuse a sense of sympathy for each of these characters. These are lives filled with human failings.

Works Cited

Iyengar, K. R. Srinivasa. *Indian Writing in English.* New Delhi: Sterling Publishers, 2010.

Site location www.cariboùsmom.com

Site location www.guardian.co.uk/bookshop

Desai, Kiran. *The Inheritance of Loss.* New Delhi: Penguin Books, 2006.

15

East-West conflict and Identity in Kiran Desai's *The Inheritance of Loss.*

Arun Kumar Mukhopadhyay

A theme of alienation and East-West conflict in general characterises the attention in Indian English Fiction by forging a co-existence of native and Western cultural principles and paradigms. But whereas the works of early writers like R.K.Narayan, Raja Rao or M.R.Anand articulate an urge for a rooted identity – for a resubmergence of the individual self to the cultural soul of the nation; writers of the present generation like Kiran Desai rather show a postcolonial angst of exile and the futility of individual aspirations in the face of an emerging world-order of migration and diasporic conditions aggravated by the cultural and economic power[s] of globalisation. Kiran Desai's problematic treatment of identity in terms of the presentation of her characters in *The Inheritance of Loss* (2006), gestures to an inexorable space for the lived experience of individuals in a multicultural world where individual will fails to negotiate the emerging reality of socio-political changes.

In *The Inheritance of Loss*, Kiran Desai's characters bear

as a cross an abortive impact of the West which leads in a way, to a poignant sense of loss – the loss of some original métier of one's existence. The main plot of the story is set in and around Darjeeling during a phase of political turbulence initiated by the Gorkhaland movement (a movement for separate statehood for the Gorkhas) in the eighties. Desai's art of characterisation in this novel is also important from the feminist point of view since the protagonist here is Sai, a teen-aged, orphaned girl who, after being brought up in a British-style boarding school in India, now comes to stay with her grandfather Jemubhai Patel, a retired judge in Cho Oyu (a crumbling hillside bungalow in Kalimpong in the northeastern Himalayas) where the grandfather is living the rest of his days with his pet dog Mutt and his old, nameless cook. In this novel, Sai, the protagonist is presented with some typical characteristics that do not belong to a 'rooted' Indian. First of all, Sai's parentage, the circumstances in which she comes to her grandfather, the only living person of her own for shelter and later her romantic affair with her Math tutor Gyan, who is another typical Indian 'subaltern' as a descendant of a Nepali Gurkha mercenary, cumulatively lend an aura of unconventionality to her character. She is born of a Zoroastrian father and a Gujarati mother and her being settled in India is only an accident. This is literally true since Sai's mother was excommunicated from her family after her marriage and both of Sai's parents died in a street accident in Moscow before she comes to her grandfather Jemubhai for shelter. Sai's education in typically British colonial system and her upbringing have bred in her a distinct socio-cultural personality that shows an utter incompatibility with any so called Indian experience and this is revealed in terms of Gyan's sentiments regarding Sai after their relationship tends to snap following the latter's involvement in the Gorkhaland movement:

> She could speak no language but English and pidgin Hindi, she could not converse with any one outside

> her tiny social stratum ... could not eat with her hands; could not squat down on the ground...had never been to a temple but for architectural interest [...]left a Bollwood film so exhausted...used paper to clean her botom; felt happier with so-called English vegetables, ... (Desai 176).

Even though the love affair between Sai and Gyan begins with the traditional or say, primeaval aspect of romanticism (' ... the first touch ... they had touched each other as if they might break' p.249), it is only natural that such a relationship with an utter incompatibility in cultural backgrounds, outlooks and a mounting mutual recrimination for each other, does not last long and their separation is paradoxically marked by a quest for identity in both of them with regard to what one represents in the eyes of the other. Gyan, is easily lured by ethnic Nepalese insurgency in favour of a separate Gorkhaland and eventually recoils from Sai. He feels himself being galvanised into the 'hero for the homeland' through his frenzied actions like filling up the jeep in the petrol pump and driving off without paying, or planning to burn the circuit house and interestingly, he is convinced that 'he owed much to the rejection of Sai' (Desai 260) since Sai now emerges in Gyan's jaundiced view, only as a superfluous relic of the rootless aristocracy or the vile and upstart upper middle-class Anglophiles, the pampered sect that has played an instrumental role in the nation's policy for disowning the *dalits* like the Gorkhas/Nepalees of their due social status in their own land and leaving them practically doubly colonised. As he says to her: "You are like slaves, that's what you are, running after the West, embarrassing yourself. It's because of people like you we never get any where" (163). On the otherhand, Gyan's involvement in the movement for separate statehood, no matter whether it is ill-directed or not, makes no sense to Sai, an Anglophile by taste and outlook and being infuriated by Gyan's growing indifference to her, she blurts out in a poignant moment in their traumatic last meeting: "You hate me [...] for reasons that have nothing to do to me" (260). Sai realises the futility of her love for Gyan: "What kind of man was this? She could not believe she has loved something so despicable. Her kiss had not turned him into a prince, he had morphed into a bloody frog" (249). Sai's pathetic anagnorisis of the emotional inanity of her existence (*'What will happen to me?!'*) is illumined by the writer's touching analysis of two alternate spaces, familial and personal, in Sai's predicament that offer no fruitful reciprocity to lead to a cohesive and reparative identity:

> Gyan would find adulthood and purity in a quest for a homeland and she would be left for ever adolescent, trapped in shameful dramatics. This was the history that sustained her: the family that never cared, the lover who forgot... .(265)

Desai has treated her major theme of migration as the 'iron law' of present-day world and 'the anxiety of being a foreigner' in the character of Biju , the son of Jemubhai's cook, in the parallel narrative of the novel. Biju, belongs to the "shadow class" of illegal immigrants in New York and passes much of his time tackling the authorities, pottering from one ill-paid job to another. Interestingly, Biju is a skilled Indian cook following his father's occupation and here too, in the presentation of Biju's bizzare existence in the States, in his desperate driftings in the basement kitchens of New York restaurants, the writer perhaps subverts the traditional concept of identity by putting the Indian *Barnashrama*[1] system to test in a different cultural space. As has been already mentioned, the predicament faced by Biju offers another facet of modern experience – immigration that '...so often presented as a heroic act, could just as easily be the opposite; "... it was cowardice that led many to America; fear marked the journey, not bravery; a cockroachy desire to scuttle to where you never saw property ...."(299). The following excerpt contains a touching irony in Biju's experience of an illegal immigrant's existence in a First world metropolis when at the Gandhi Cafe in New York, he is overcome by self-pity after breaking his leg and receiving no medical attention from his employer Harish Harry:

> Looking at a dead insect in the sack of basmati that had come all the way from Dehra Dun, he almost wept in sorrow and marvelled at its journey, which was tenderness for his own journey. In India almost nobody would be able to afford this rice, and you had to travel around the world to be able to eat such things where they were cheap enough that you could gobble them down without being rich; and when you got home to the place where they grew, you couldn't afford them anymore. (191)

Biju's decision to go home after all, at this ironic moment of self-assertion, is a marker of a deliberate bid of expiation following an epiphany of a reparative identity out of his designated subject-position in the First World. His experience of the businessmen's eating steak and exulting over the wealth to be exacted from the new markets of Asia justifiably makes him "a man full to the brim with a wish to live within a narrow purity". (137) For a poor and lonely outsider like him, the city's endless possibilities for self-invention become a source of angst, a space where the culture of justice lies at the hands of a privileged few. It is significant that though "another part of him had expanded: his self-consciousness, his self-pity," this awareness only makes him long for the acquisition of a reparative identity – to return "to where he might relinquish this overrated control over his own destiny". (268) He comes back with a wish to begin anew: "...the enormous anxiety of being a foreigner ebbing – that unbearable arrogance and shame of the immigrant. He looked about and for the first time in God knows how long, his vision unblurred and he found that he could see properly". (300)

However, his return to his country is not edifying in the context of his suffering from the local eruptions of rage, fits of corruptions and frustration in the land gruelling under the pledge for self-status – such repurcussions that he was physically unacquainted with in U.S.A. Though the re-union scene between a demented father and a dispossessd, America - returned son in the closing lines of the book offers a streak of hope, a resemblance to some possibility ("The five peaks of Kanchenjangha turned golden with the kind of luminous light that made you feel, if briefly, that truth was apparent" p.324); the writer's valedictory statement ("All you needed to do was to reach out and pluck it".) is equally imbued with a sense of inexorability of experience in this globalised, multiplex form of cultural identity (signified by 'five peaks') in this modern, post-colonial world where individual choice and mind-set of the common man with rooted sensibilities is too weak an armour to encounter the disruptive whirls of change.

Whereas the chracters in the works of Narayan and Rao show an active and fruitful urge for a rooted and autonomous identity in the matrix of their re-invented tradition and their creators show, to quote Meenakshi Mukherjee, "the anxiety of Indianness"[2] in the face of postcolonial hybridity; for Biju and the others like Sai or even Gyan (who alone in the novel shows, though upto a limit, an active urge for an authentic identity as per his own conviction), Desai offers in the ultimate reckoning, no possibility of total withdrawal, escape, or reintegration. The intransigence of purpose in Gyan (similar to Yeats's diagnosis of Maud Gonne's refusal of the poet's love for her in the poem "Easter 1916":'Too long a sacrifice/ Can make a stone of the heart', Line –57-58) that has impelled him to sacrifice his love, ultimately slackens as the readers find that Gyan decides to moderate his militancy under the guile of practical intelligence, of restraint or care for his family since his authoritarian grandmother does not approve his desperadoes in favour of the GNLF movement.

The emerging reality of a slow attitudinal change in now circumspect Gyan has been ironically traced by the writer:

> [...] timidity might be disguised, well, in a perfectly ordinary existence situated between meek contours. Saved from one humiliation by being horrible to Sai, he could now be serendipitously saved from another by claiming respect for his grandmother. Cowardice needed its façade, its reasoning, like anything else if it was to be his life's principle. Contentment was no easy matter. One had to situate it cannily, camouflage it, pretend it was something else.[...]. Pleasures existed in the world - intense, tiny pleasures that nevertheless created a feeling of space on all sides. (272-73)

For Sai too, analysis of her lived experiences reveals contradictory spaces that fail to offer to her 'self' any satisfactory interaction, any positive meaning, any system of surviving values or roots, so to say, that she can rely upon to etch out a meaningful identity:

> "What is this all about?" asked Sai, but her mouth could not address her ear ... her heart lying in pieces, did not seem able to address her mind; her mind could not talk to her heart. " Shame on myself..."she said...who was she ... she with her self-importance, her demand for happiness, yelling it at fate, at the deaf heavens, screaming for her joy to be brought forth... ?(322)

The same vein of fatalism continues in her final judgement of her own experiences where emotions writhe in the blind alley of desire baffling her education, faith and understanding. Desai has perfectly caught the stream of consciousness in Sai's conclusive diagnosis of her own predicament:

> Her small greedy soul [...]. Her tantrums and fits. [...]. Her mean tears [...].Her crying, enough for

> all the sadness in the world, was only for herself. Life was not single in its purpose [...] or even in its direction. [...].The simplicity of what she'd been taught wouldn't hold. Never again could she think there was but one narrative and that this narrative belonged only to herself, that she might create her own mean little happiness and live safely within it. (323)

The case of Jemubhai Patel offers a different version of identity-formation, the phenomenon of *Trishanku*[3] state where a blind quest for appropriation of mainstream British culture to the exclusion of indigenous cultural roots, causes a distinctive cultural amnesia in a section of upper-middleclass, so-called bourgeoise Indians. The judge is therefore one of those footloose, rootless and "ridiculous Indians," as the writer puts it, "who couldn't rid themselves of what they had broken their souls to learn" and whose Anglophilia can only turn into self-hatred. Desai has stressed the irony in Jemubhai's affected, self-exoticised existence: "He was a foreigner - a foreigner – every bit of him screamed. Only his digestion dissented and told him that he was home: squatting painfully in that cramped outhouse, his gentleman's knees creaking, swearing "Bloody hell", he felt his digestion work as super efficient as—as *Western transportation*" (166-67).

Even to some of Desai's other and rather minor characters who live in the neighbourhood of Jemubhai in Kalimpong, the changes caused by socio-political/ethnic issues in the Himalayas evokes mixed responses though all these changes as a rule, look forward to some uncertainty, some loss of sustenance. To Lola Banerjee, a widowed aristocrat (who is convinced "Gorkhas are merceneries, that's what they are"), things have shocking repurcussions and the writer traces Lola's experiences of a futile effort to extricate a portion of her French-styled residence Mon Ami from encroachment by some local GNLF rowdies: "Just when Lola had thought it would continue, a hundred years like the one past - Trollope,

BBC, a burst of hilarity at Christmas - all of a sudden, all that they had claimed innocent, fun, funny, not really to matter, was proven wrong". (241-42) Noni, Lola's sister, who is slightly sympathetic to the insurgents ("...there is some truth to what they are saying. Gorkhas have been used ...") and believes that "in any such situation the atrocities are committed under the cover of a legitimate cause', nevertheless detects a practice of doubleness that fails to cope with the fluidity, an unauthentication of space for their living as Desai has aptly described:

> The real place had evaded them. The two of them had been fools feeling they were doing something exciting just by occupying this picturesque cottage, by seducing themselves with those old travel books in the library [...]. Parallel lives were being led by those - Budhoo, Kesang - for whom there was no such doubleness or self-consciousness, while Lola and Noni indulged themselves in the pretense of it being a daily fight to keep up civilization in this place of towering, flickering green. (247)

In the eyes of Mrs.Sen, a neighbour of Lola and Noni, whose daughter Munmun is a green card holder in the States and now working in the CNN, the change has only a skin-deep effect which is symptomatic of an absence of rootedness: "what was a country but the idea of it? She thought of India as a concept, a hope, or a desire". (236) Even the nameless cook, Biju's father, who lives a life of indignity dreaming solely of Biju's well-being, fails to negotiate the abrupt change in his familiar space as he experiences the July 27 Uprising for Gorkhaland in 1986. Crawling his way back to Cho Oyu, hiding in the bushes in fear of the petrolling Army, the cook has the following revelation that points to the de-stabilising effect of modern socio-political movements upon the poor, simple and unsophisticated souls who face an identity-crisis, a state of '*swagrihe parabasi*' condition (feeling alienated at home) that operates both at the level of community consciousness and blood-relation:

> This place, the market where he had bargained contentedly over potatoes and insulted, yes insulted the fruit wallah with happy impunity, [...] this place where he had resided secure in the knowledge that this was basically a civilized place where there was room for them all, [...] – was showing him now that he had been wrong. He wasn't wanted at Kalimpong and he did not belong.

At this moment, a fear overtook him that he might never see his son again –

> The letters that had come all these years were only his own hope writing to him. Biju was just a habit of thought. He didn't exist.Could he? (278)

As a diasporic writer hererself, who had left India at the age of 14 and now living in the States on a student-visa, Kiran Desai's concept of 'nation' may very well proximate to that of Mrs.Sen, one of her characters, as merely an 'idea', 'a concept, a hope, or a desire' and thereby may corroborate to Anderson's celebrated idea of nation as an "imagined community"[4]. The writer's presentation of different faces of diasporic experiences (for example, of Lola, Noni and other Indians in their own country and of an Indian like Biju in a foreign country), seems to suggest that this trauma of rootlessnes is more psychological than geographic in its impact upon the individuals. Living without the self-sufficient and sustaining systems in one's own tradition, the norms or values endorsed by the indigenous culture, underscores the destiny of the once colonised people in this modern, postcolonial world, no matter whether they live at home or abroad. A critic like Satiș Shroff has criticised Kiran as 'a supercilious brown-memsahib', and her idea of the nation as theoretical and superficial:

What is missing in her writing is the intercultural

competence. Instead of taking the trouble to learn Nepali and acquiring background knowledge about the tradition, religion, norms and values, culture and living style of the Gorkhalis in Darjeeling and the Nepalese in Nepal, and comparing it with her own Indian culture, and trying to seek what is common between the two cultures and moving towards peace, tolerance, reconciliation – she just remains adamant, like her protagonist Sai. She does not make an ethnic reflection, but goes on and on, with a jaundiced view, till the bitter end. (Shroff, *para* 14)

However, this is exactly the area which marks the cross-over point between life and art in this novel which articulates through the characters like Biju, the literal, subjective truth of the writer – the 'anxiety of being a foreigner', though in an aesthetic self-distancing mode. In fact, this artistic incorporation of the writer's real-life experiences into literary discourse., endorses here the literary endeavour for cultural documentation from the feminist point of view. The constant shift between insurgency in India and the immigrant experience in New York or the alternation of the two plot-components in the novel not only develops the story, but also shapes the narrative perspective of situating the postcolonial trauma of migration or rootlessness in a multicultural or a globalised context. The novel documents the writer's view of modernity as an unhappy tryst between past and present effecting a sort of psychological migration in the individuals to whom modernity stands for a continuous menace to their ideals of right, justice or dignity which is projected as the onus of common inheritance.

In fact, the fictional strategy here by presenting a hermeneutics of loss and nostalgia, rather subscribes, strategically speaking, to Bruce King's concept of the 'politics of ambivalence' in the entire postcolonial project that seems to create "conditions for appropriation and resistance from the moments of its impact, and to recognise how superficial the exigencies of political change and independence may have been in bringing the need for resistance and change to a satisfactory conclusion" (King 165).

NOTES

1. The trditional system that approves the adoption of one's hereditary occupation. As per traditional Hinduism, the Barna system, also known as varnashrama dharma, is based on principles laid down in the scriptures of the Vedic tradition, which categorize Hindus into four "varnas" or social classes and prescribe specific duties for each. These are the brahmanas (*brahmins*) (serving as priests and teachers), kshatriyas (duties of administration, battle, and law enforcement), vaishyas (customarily agriculture, commerce, and cow-protection), and shudras (who provide service to members of the other three varnas). In this system, it is the brahmins and not the kings, who commanded the greatest respect in society despite their relative lack of wealth or political power. Implicit within the concept is the idea that most Hindus would faithfully follow their prescribed duties for the greater good of the entire society. Emphasis added.
2. The expression is originally taken from the title of a chapter in Meenakshi Mukherjee's book *The Perishable Empire* (2000). According to Sujala Singh, here the writer with this expression 'articulates a characteristic scepticism towards the perceived globalising trend in post-colonial Indian writing: 'The Indian novelists to be taken seriously are the ones not conditioned by the pressures of the global market.' (Singh, *para* 2) To put it simply in relevance to our discussion, this 'anxiety of Indianness' characterises the acquisition of identity in the nationalist writers of the colonial period like Narayan or Rao which betrays a tension, an ambivalence between traditional binds of native culture and dialectical pulls of the Western; between tradition on the one hand and modernity on the other.
3. Trishanku is the character in Hindu mythology.

Trishanku is commonly referred to through the phrase "Trishanku's heaven". The phrase describes a middleground or a compromise between ones goals or desires and one's current state or possessions. The story of Trishanku is told in the Bala Kanda portion of the Valmiki Ramayana.Trishanku, the son of Prithu was a king in the Solar Dynasty, the dynasty of the great Hindu God Rama. Trishanku wished to ascend to heaven in his mortal body and requested his Guru Vasishta to perform the needful rites to achieve this goal. Vasishta refused for it was against the laws of nature for a mortal to enter heaven. Upon refusal, Trishanku approached the sons of Vasishta to help him. The request of Trishanku in spite of the refusal by their father angered the sons of Vasishta and they cursed Trishanku with a debilitating disease. Trishanku was forced to leave his country and wander the lands.

4. Anderson in his book *Imagined Community* (1938), confers an 'imagined', not any geographic status on 'nation' and writes that "the members of even the smallest nation will never know most of their fellow members, ...yet in the mind of each lives the image of their communion'.(p.15)

Works Cited

Anderson, Benedict. *Imagined Community: Reflections on the Origin and Spread of Nationalism*. London:Verso, 1938.

Desai, Kiran. *The Inheritance of Loss*. New Delhi: Penguin Books, 2006.

King, Bruce. *The New National and Post-colonial Literatures: An Introduction*. New York: OUP, 1996.

Mukherjee, Meenakshi. *The Perishable Empire: Essays on Indian Writing in English*. New Delhi: OUP (Paperback), 2002.

Shroff, Satis. "Kathmandu Blues: 'The Inheritance of Loss' and Intercultural Competence". 07.01.2007.

http:www.americanchronicle.com/articles/view/18756

Singh, Sujala. "Who Can Save the Subaltern? Knowledge and Power in Amitav Ghosh's the Circle of Reason": Critical Survey, Vol. 16, 2004.

20.04.09.<<http:www.questia.comgoogleScholar,qst;jsessionid=>>

Yeats, William Butler. "Easter 1916": *W.B.Yeats: Selected Poetry*. Ed. A. Norman Jeffers. Kolkata: Radha Publishing House, 1989.

Index